## Communicating with pattern

# Stripes

RotoVision

Published and distributed by RotoVision SA
Route Suisse 9, CH-1295, Mies, Switzerland
RotoVision SA Sales and Editorial Office
Sheridan House, 114 Western Road, Hove
BN3 1DD UK
Tel: + 44 (0) 1273 72 72 68
Fax: + 44 (0) 1273 72 72 69
Email: sales@rotovision.com
Web: www.rotovision.com

10 9 8 7 6 5 4 3 2 1
ISBN: 2-940361-15-0

Original book concept: Luke Herriott
and Keith Stephenson.
Art director for RotoVision: Tony Seddon
Design and artwork: Keith and Spike
at Absolute Zero Degrees
Additional illustrations: Keith Stephenson

Printed in Singapore by Star Standard
Industries (Pte)Ltd

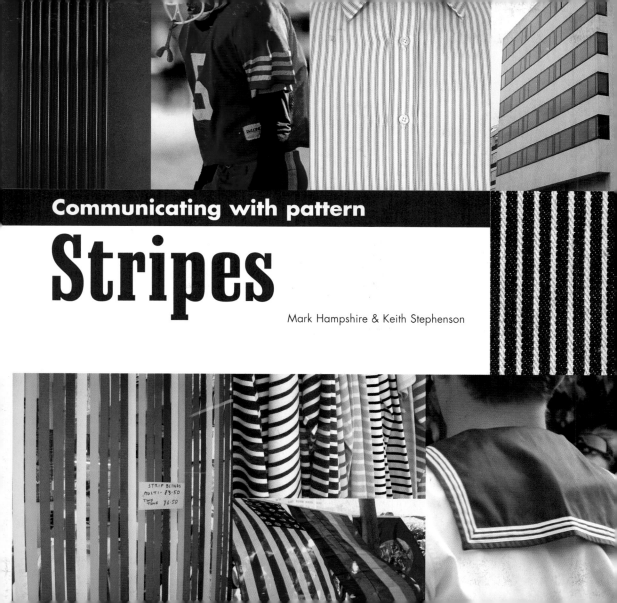

# Communicating with pattern

# Stripes

Mark Hampshire & Keith Stephenson

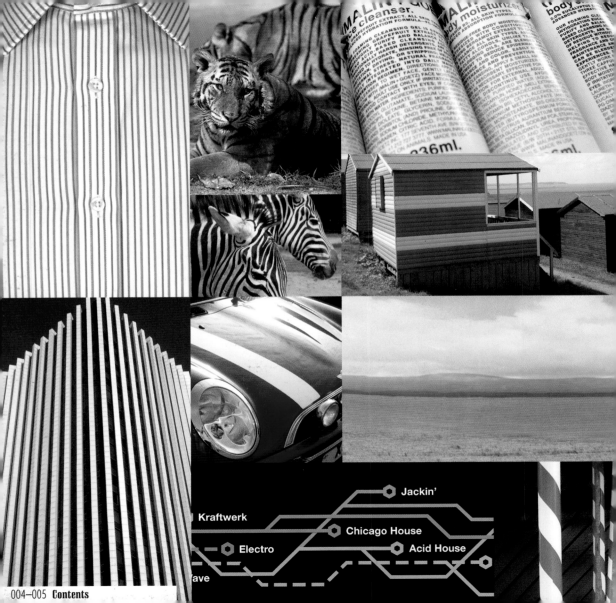

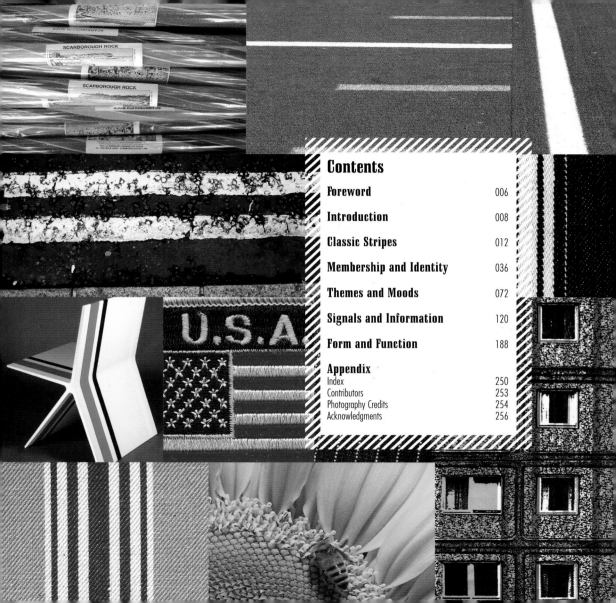

# Contents

# Foreword

Stripes on walls, stripes on floors, stripes on columns, stripes on roads, stripes on clothes, stripes on art, stripes in nature, stripes on flags, go-faster stripes, stripes to mark hazards, stripes on the Josephine Baker House by Adolph Loos, Daniel Buren stripes, Sybila Berger stripes, Jim Lambie stripes, Ellsworth Kelly stripes. Stripes can come in handy.

Stripes are some of my favorite things.

Stripes communicate many things. Mostly they draw attention to whatever they are applied to. I could never have predicted the impact that painting stripes on columns in The Haçienda nightclub would have in 1982. The image of stripes on columns in The Haçienda has bounced around the globe and have reappeared in too many appropriated settings to mention.

**Stripe n**. *Long narrow band or strip on surface from which it differs in colour or texture (STARS and Stripes); (Mil.) chevron etc. denoting rank; type of character, opinion, etc. (a man of that stripe)*

Definition taken from **The Pocket Oxford Dictionary**.

Abstract, sociological, militarist, instructional, decorative, natural, anthropological. Stripes are like an extrusion, you cut them off as and where you need them, long or short, wide or narrow, vertical, horizontal, or at an angle. Stripes to fit any occasion.

Black and yellow stripes are the best.

**Ben Kelly**

*001 Daniel Buren—Photo-souvenir:*
*"Peinture aux formes indéfinies" July 1966, Paris*

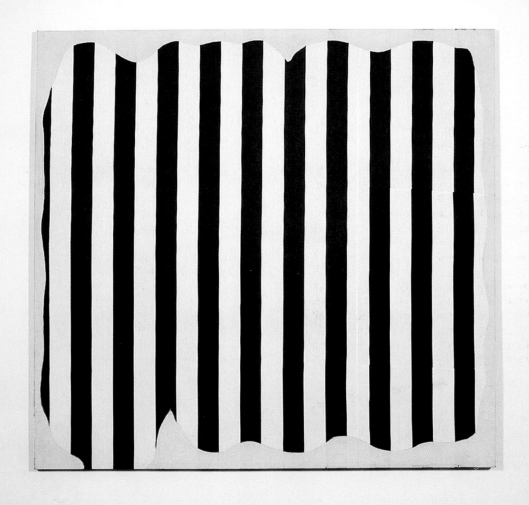

# Introduction

Stripes are one of the most widely used and enduring of patterns. Timeless, gender neutral, and appealing to all ages, they are a highly versatile communication tool. While they are perhaps the simplest of design motifs, stripes create maximum impact. Their ability to highlight a feature or distinguish specific areas comes from the high contrast that is achieved by juxtaposing colors, textures, or materials in simple lines, straight or curved. Stripes seem to shout louder than other patterns. Elegant, playful, or brash, stripes always make their presence felt. This degree of impact is used to great effect by designers and artists in a contemporary context where anything that offers visual cut-through, differentiation, or individuality is a good thing. But it hasn't always been that way.

Stripes single out the wearer, the room, the car—whatever they adorn—and say: "notice me!" In previous centuries, being marked out as different meant exclusion from society—being branded an outsider. Stripes do a good job of this. Paleographer Michel Pastoureau, has made a study of the historical and social significance of the stripe and the problems it has caused society through the centuries. The medieval eye regarded the stripe as something to be mistrusted because it interrupts any sense of visual harmony. Perhaps this is why, throughout the Middle Ages, the stripe was reserved for the social outcast. Prostitutes, prisoners, jugglers, even the Devil have all been either forced to wear stripes or have been depicted wearing stripes.

Over the past two centuries, though, the stripe has gained respectability, finding alternative uses and new significance. Once a mark of shame, stripes have performed a volte-face and are now awarded to signify achievement, rank, or status, or chosen to adorn smart, sophisticated suits. Even present-day applications of stripes that signify something bad, like hazard stripes, have a warning function that benefits society. →

*002* The Paul Smith special edition Mini, launched at the Tokyo Motor Show, 1997.

→ Today, interpretations of the stripe can be as rich and diverse as the society in which it operates. Stripes can be fun, elegant, sporty, nautical, daring, or brash. It is this diversity that makes the stripe so interesting for artists, fashion designers, architects, and graphic designers. In the art world, renowned figures such as Daniel Buren, Bridget Riley, and Mark Rothko have all included stripes in their work, each exploring different visual and emotional territories. Think of stripes in fashion, and Paul Smith, agnès b, and Missoni immediately come to mind—again, each uses stripes to achieve a very individual esthetic. And the stripe isn't confined to the world of applied pattern. Stripes can be formed by the vertical lines of classical columns, by the molded contours of a contemporary chair, or abstracted from a living landscape.

Imagine a simple rectangular box. Paint it with bold vertical stripes in red, white, and green and it becomes packaging for anything Italian, perhaps pasta. Paint it black with three white stripes and it contains a pair of Adidas sneakers. Print it with a striped barcode and it holds all the information required to swipe, purchase, and take away.

**Communicating with Pattern: Stripes** explores the language of this graphic pattern. Each chapter looks at different applications, showing stripes in situ and showcasing design work that features stripes. It's a visual mood board that will inspire you to experiment with the range of communication opportunities that stripes offer. It explores the classics that have become part of our everyday lives and looks at how stripes can define identity and membership. It offers a broad range of themes and moods that can be expressed through stripes and pays tribute to hard working stripes that are used as signals and to convey information. Finally, it uncovers the more esoteric stripes that are part of the form and function of structures and the environment.

When you communicate with stripes you find endless possibilities. With this book, we hope to redefine expectations of this humble pattern, to show stripes in unexpected places, doing unexpected jobs, and creating an impact you never thought possible.

**003** Pioneers of hip-hop music, Run DMC also introduced hip-hop style to the world. Run (born Joseph Simmons), his friends Darryl McDaniels and Jason Mizell (alias Jam Master Jay) distinguished themselves from other bands not only by their beats and lyrics, but also by creating an iconic street look that reflected the style of the Queens neighborhood where they grew up. It is celebrated here by Adidas in the "Superstar 35" series.

# Classic Stripes

Pinstripes
Striped Shirts
Breton Stripes
Cornish Ware
Ticking
Regency Stripes

007

008

009

011

01

014—015 **Classic Stripes**

## Classic Stripes

Classic stripes are those that touch our everyday lives, the ones that spring to mind because they have official "stripe" names, like pinstripes or Regency stripes. They are the most enduring of stripes, often bearing cultural or historical significance.

Falling largely into garment stripes and domestic stripes, these classics encompass the two main media for striped application—our clothes and our homes. These are stripes that society has come to depend on to communicate particular messages or perform specific tasks: the Breton shirt, beloved of beatniks and fashionistas; the shirting stripe, marking out high business achievers; the Regency stripe, bringing order and sophistication to a room.

Here we give credit to bold stripes that identify, elegant stripes that reassure, crisp stripes that comfort, and vulgar stripes that disturb. All have earned a place in our everyday visual vocabulary; all have become classics in their own right.

**004** *Ticking stripe by Ian Mankin, UK.*
**005** *Pinstriped suit by Paul Smith, UK.*
**006** *Striped shirt by Thomas Pink, UK.*
**007** *Classic Regency striped wallpaper.*
**008** *Pinstriped suit by Paul Smith, UK.*
**009** *Striped shirt by Thomas Pink, UK.*
**010** *Cornish Ware by T.G. Green, UK.*
**011** *Striped T-shirts by agnès b, France.*
**012** *Pinstriped fabric by Fox Brothers, UK.*
**013** *Selection of striped fabrics by Ian Mankin, UK.*

# Pinstripes

The pinstriped suit is considered smart, elegant, for some, the height of respectability, and yet the pinstripe remains one of the most commonly misunderstood of stripes. According to which source you believe, its origins lie in opposing camps.

The conservative view is that pinstripes are sober, reliable stripes, which have their origins in the striped pants that City bankers used to wear with a morning coat. Individual banks would identify themselves by the different stripes of the pants. Eventually, the stripes were applied to the entire suit and the ubiquitous City uniform was born. All very plausible, especially when viewed from the 21st century perspective that pinstripes represent everything that is conservative, even a little staid, in the world of business and finance.

Other sources refute this idea. The opposing theory is that the true origin of the pinstripe is the boating suit of the 1890s. The early 20th century saw an explosion of pattern and self-expression in men's clothing, and the pinstripe was probably a rather showy alternative to other, more somber options. With its roots in sportswear, not business attire, the pinstripe was a liberating force rather than a constraining uniform of the establishment. Given the fact that the pinstripe was adopted by the likes of Al Capone, it seems credible that its first outing was more about in-your-face shock value than unassuming conformity.

More confusion arises over what actually constitutes a pinstripe. Technically, pinstripes are fine stripes made up of pinhead-sized dots of yarn in the warp of a worsted fabric. The distinction is not always made between it and the chalk stripe—a rather more gauche affair with a thicker stripe woven into a flannel, where the fabric is milled to create a fuzzy effect. The lace-line stripe is made up of several pinheads in a row, and the rope stripe is a broader stripe again, woven in a diagonal fashion to create a spiral stripe. →

**014** A traditional pinstriped suit.
**015–024** A selection of pinstripes and chalk stripes currently in production from Fox Brothers, UK, developed from their archive of woven fabrics, which dates back 230 years.

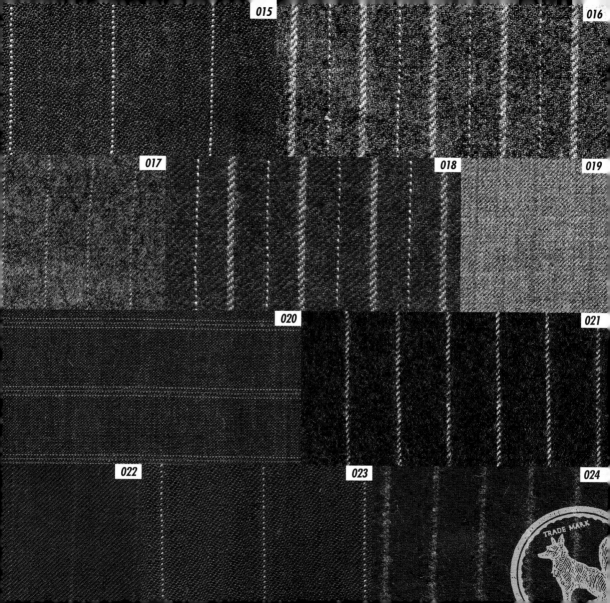

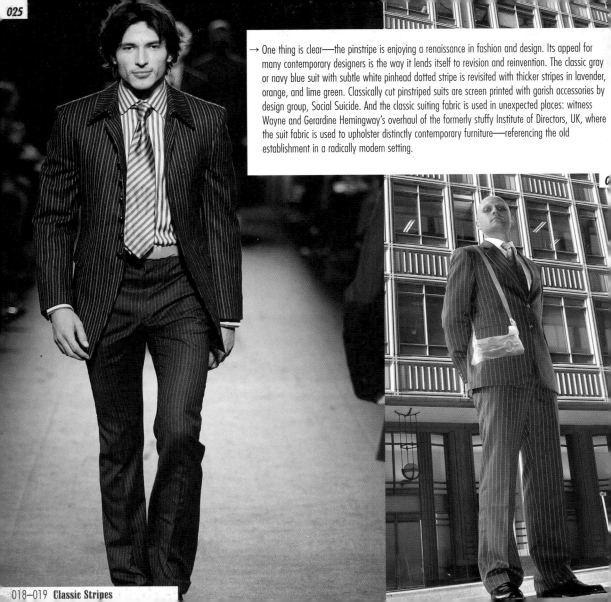

→ One thing is clear—the pinstripe is enjoying a renaissance in fashion and design. Its appeal for many contemporary designers is the way it lends itself to revision and reinvention. The classic gray or navy blue suit with subtle white pinhead dotted stripe is revisited with thicker stripes in lavender, orange, and lime green. Classically cut pinstriped suits are screen printed with garish accessories by design group, Social Suicide. And the classic suiting fabric is used in unexpected places: witness Wayne and Gerardine Hemingway's overhaul of the formerly stuffy Institute of Directors, UK, where the suit fabric is used to upholster distinctly contemporary furniture—referencing the old establishment in a radically modern setting.

"We used pinstripes in a soft furnishing fabric on the seating in the IOD at 123 Pall Mall project as a playful nod to the city business heritage of the Institute of Directors, and also as a reference to the fact that this was the first project outside of the fashion industry for Hemingway Design."

*Wayne Hemingway,*
*Hemingway Design, UK*

**025** Classic pinstripes with a twist by Paul Smith, UK.
**026** Social Suicide, UK, subvert the pinstripe by screen printing a traditional suit with a glamorous shoulder bag on their "Lovely" jacket.
**027** Playful yet respectable: the Institute of Directors interior by Hemingway Design, UK.

## Striped Shirts

Often seen as the favored shirt of the banker, lawyer, and accountant, the striped shirt is almost a demographic identifier. Much as "blue collar" and "white collar" categorized the late 20th century workforce, so now, we have the "striped collar" professional. That decade of conspicuous excess, the 1980s, was largely responsible for the re-emergence of the striped shirt in business—think Gordon Gekko, the uncompromising trader played by Michael Douglas in the movie *Wall Street*.

The business clichés might have faded (lunch is no longer considered for wimps) but the striped shirts haven't—in fact, judging from the success of pioneers like Thomas

Pink, they are now more popular than ever. They come in a dazzling range of styles, with the stripes—always running vertically—varying from the simple: one color on white, to the exuberant: vividly contrasting stripes of many colors in varying widths.

You'll also find stripes worn in more casual work environments such as the creative and media industries. Here, though, the stripe of choice is a more casual affair—sports influenced, with a mildly retro appeal. Designer Toby Bradbury noticed their prevalence amongst his colleagues and created a photo diary of all the different striped shirts around him from day to day.

*028–045 Thomas Pink, UK, was established in the 18th century, originally manufacturing hunting jackets. To wear one was to be "in the pink"—hence the well-known phrase. Relaunched in the 1980s, they have become known around the world for their classic striped shirts—now available for men and women.*

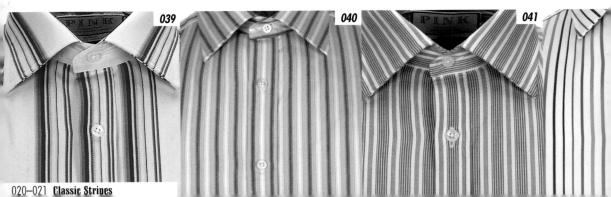

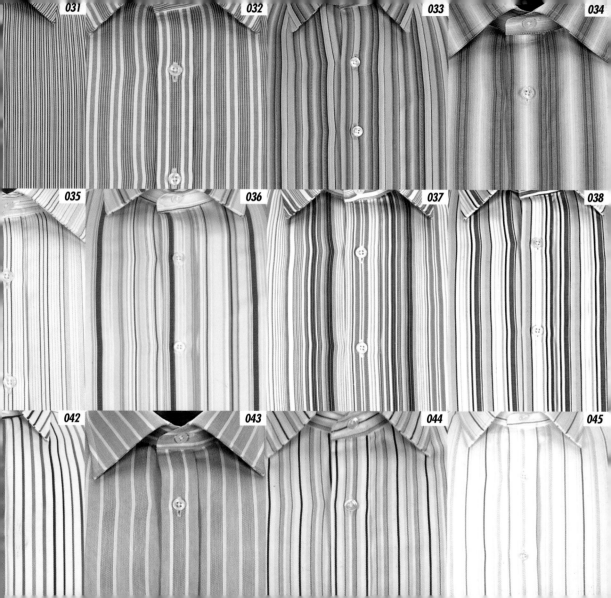

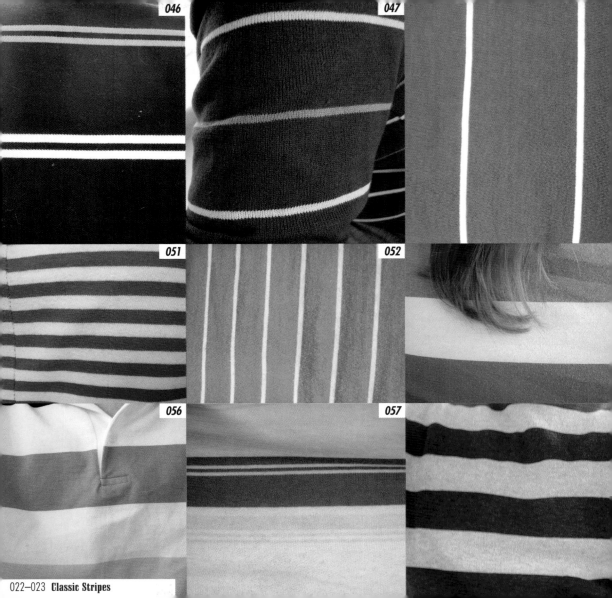

046

047

051

052

056

057

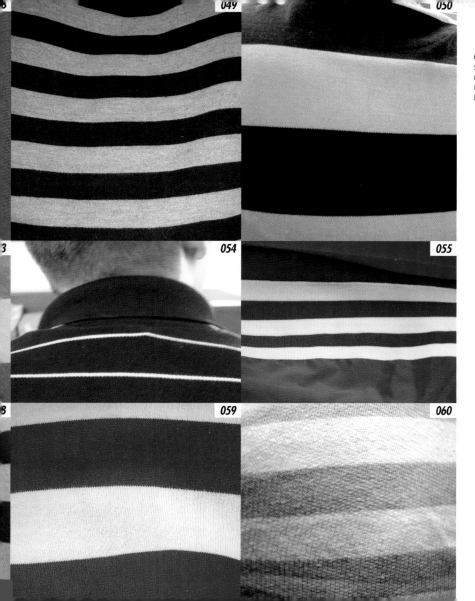

**046–060** The alternative business stripe. Toby Bradbury took these pictures at his workplace over a period of time, visually logging the diversity of stripes being worn to work by his colleagues.

## Breton Stripes

In France, the traditional striped fisherman's shirt is commonly referred to as a *chandail*, named after the 18th century French onion merchants (in French, *marchand d'ail* means garlic seller) who sailed to England from the shores of Brittany. They wore striped garments to stand out when selling their wares—so the *chandail* was an early form of branding and advertising. But where do these stripes come from?

Naval stripes have been in existence since the 17th century. Junior French naval recruits wore a striped T-shirt for the first three months of their training. Because these stripes signified a member of the crew rather than a captain, they can be seen as having a derogatory effect on the wearer. Perhaps this is why anti-establishment figures often adopt these commoners' stripes: they are popular with artists, musicians, eccentrics, and *enfants terribles*. Think of famous pictures of Picasso and Jean Paul Gaultier looking mischievous in traditional stripy chandails.

**061** Traditional Breton striped shirts available for eccentrics and enfants terribles from The Original Breton Shirt Company, UK.

**062** "Le Male" men's fragrance by Jean Paul Gaultier. Its packaging celebrates the traditional Breton stripe and complements the women's fragrance range.

**063** Souvenir of the Breton region: a tin bearing the Breton flag stripes.

But for all their enduring popularity, the true origins of Breton stripes remain unclear. Were the onion sellers the first to adopt them? Are they rooted in the region's naval history? Are they linked to the traditional Breton flag, which bears five black stripes on a white background? One thing is certain: to the rest of the world, these striped T-shirts and sweaters in ecru with blue, black, or red stripes are unequivocally French.    →

"Stripes have been part of my universe forever. The origin of them in my collections is related to my childhood and to the culture surrounding me. When I was little, my sister and I used to be dressed up in little T-shirts and matching shorts in white and red stripes. My father wore pin-striped shirts— probably why I include them in my collections in new color palettes each season. Then growing up, my interest in cinematographic and graphic culture (Godard, Seberg) kept stripes around me. Stripes have become an emblematic design, never dated, a must-have."

*agnès b,*
*France.*

→ *Marchand* or *méchant*, agnès b exploits the duality of these stripes in her collections. Since the first boutique opened in 1975 (followed by a fortuitous meeting with a manufacturer of French rugby shirts), she has used them in different color combinations each season. In her hands, they can be elegant or edgy, according to the fashion mix. Her striped T-shirts seem to embrace the confusion between establishment and rebellion: styled as preppy/nautical or punk/new wave. But beneath this anarchic sense of playfulness there is order. The designer herself is extremely meticulous about these stripes, stressing the importance of proportions. You can recognize the genuine agnès b article by its stripes of regular measurements—either 1.2/1.2cm or 6/6cm.

**064–068** *Stripes make a perennial appearance in the men's, women's, and children's collections by agnès b. The designer's affection for the stripe goes back to her childhood.*

# Cornish Ware

"For kitchen uses it would be difficult to suggest anything cleaner looking, more truly fit for the purpose, or more delightful," said a writer in the *Pottery Gazette* in 1932 of the now legendary blue and white striped Cornish Ware from T.G. Green. It remains today a classic homeware range, collected by devotees all round the world, with rare pieces fetching in excess of $2,000. The quote says it all: the design has been at home in the kitchen for 80 years and it surely owes its enduring appeal to its "culinary" stripes, which are at once both crisp and fresh, yet warm and comforting.

Since the range has always been produced in South Derbyshire, the name Cornish Ware seems like an misnomer. Nobody knows for sure how the range got its name. Legend has it that a sales representative in the 1930s named it after "the blue of the Cornish skies and the white crests of the waves." The origins of the design are less romantic. The long established pottery, T.G. Green, needed to find employment for turners after WWI. The range is still produced by turning the pieces on a lathe—cutting away the blue slip to reveal the white ware beneath. This gives the pieces their distinctive raised bands of blue.

Cornish Ware has been imitated and even become a generic: it adorns tables in cereal commercials, its blue and white stripes are emulated on margarine tubs, art directors use it to communicate happy domesticity. This stripe owes its success to its slow pace of change. Little has altered since Royal College of Art graduate, Judith Onions, redesigned the shapes in the 1960s. Only now is the range being revisited. Under the dynamic new ownership of the Tabletop Company, new stripes in pastels, sage, and bold black and white are being launched to maintain the appeal of this timeless design.

**BREAD**

**TEA**

**UTENSILS**

**PASTA**

**CUTLERY**

**DRAINER**

**069–074** *Cornish Ware, originally developed by T.G. Green, was revitalized in the 1960s by Judith Onions and sold in the newly launched lifestyle store Habitat. Today it is produced in its traditional blue and a series of fresh new colors by the Tabletop Company, UK.*

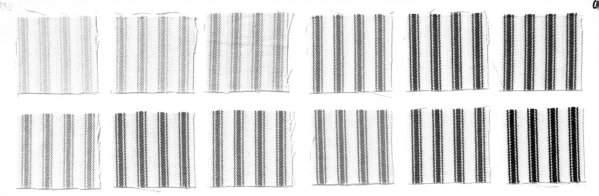

## Ticking

Used since the 1700s to upholster mattresses and cover pillows, ticking is a sturdy white or ecru fabric with a contrasting single color stripe. Simple, clean, and functional, ticking is as comforting as striped pajamas, as hygienic as striped underwear, and its stripes seem to have developed along similar principles. Originally only considered morally tolerable in "pure" white or ecru, when color was introduced to such items, it was in the form of a stripe—acceptable because it retains the integrity of the white or un-dyed fabric.

The cultural significance of the hygienic stripe might have diminished (nowadays we sleep under sheets of any color and pattern, rarely in pajamas, without losing sleep about the moral implications) but the appeal of ticking endures. A smart ticking mattress feels infinitely more pristine than one bearing flowers, geometric patterns, or garish swirls. Because it is a classic design, ticking is all you need to represent a mattress graphically. Peter Saville's cover for Suede's *Coming Up* puts the mattress center stage—a foil for an implied set of complicated relationships and encounters, creating an air of louche decadence. →

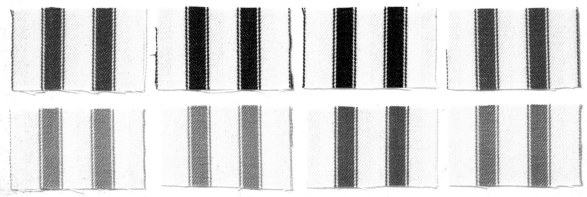

suede

Coming Up

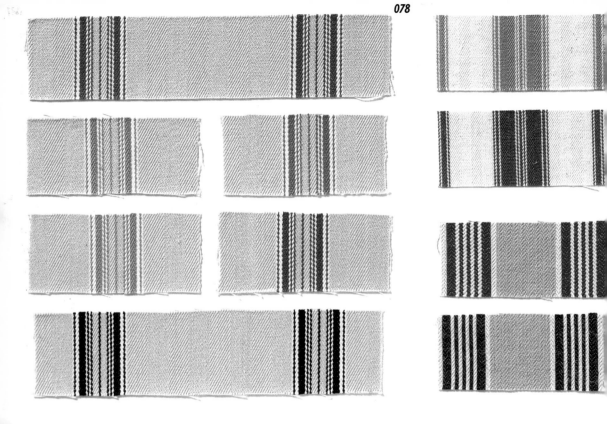

→ Now the ticking stripe has graduated from the mattress (and the bedroom) onto other items of soft furnishing. Given its popularity, it's ironic to think that it had become almost unavailable until stripe pioneer, designer Ian Mankin, set up his London stores 20 years ago, purveying good quality, affordable utility fabrics in stripes and checks. A traditionalist who can't abide faddishness, Mankin designs his stripes drawing on a lifetime of studying the detail of everyday objects like mattresses—from those in French hotel rooms to the one he slept on at boarding school.

Starting with the basic black and ecru, Ian Mankin offered traditional ticking in a range of coordinating, non-traditional colors, making the fabric more versatile for a broader range of applications. While they appear simple in concept, these stripes take a lot more thought and consideration than you might think. The spacing, the colors, and the proportions of stripe to white (or "negative") space are all crucial to creating a ticking of excellence.

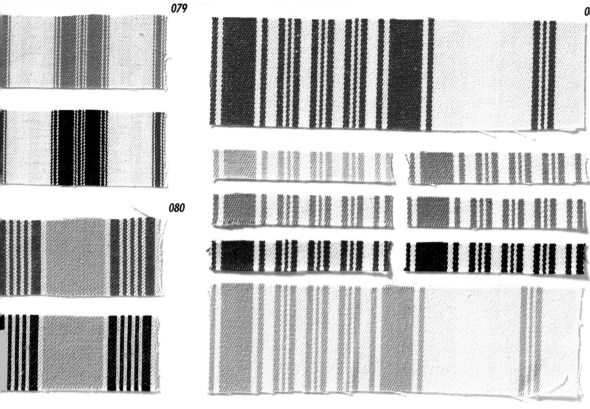

This attention to detail is surely what makes ticking so alluring. What was a utility basic now represents the epitome of understated elegance. The functional has become something stylish and covetable: to upholster a chair, festoon a window, or cover a cushion.

**075 and 076** *Traditional tickings in two sizes of stripe, designed by Ian Mankin, inspired by mattresses he's observed throughout his life.*
**077** *"Coming Up" by UK band Suede, with cover by Peter Saville, turns the humble ticking mattress into a cool icon.*

**078–081** *Variations on a theme: these tickings by Ian Mankin may seem less traditional but are still designed to his meticulous standards, with particular attention to proportion and color.*

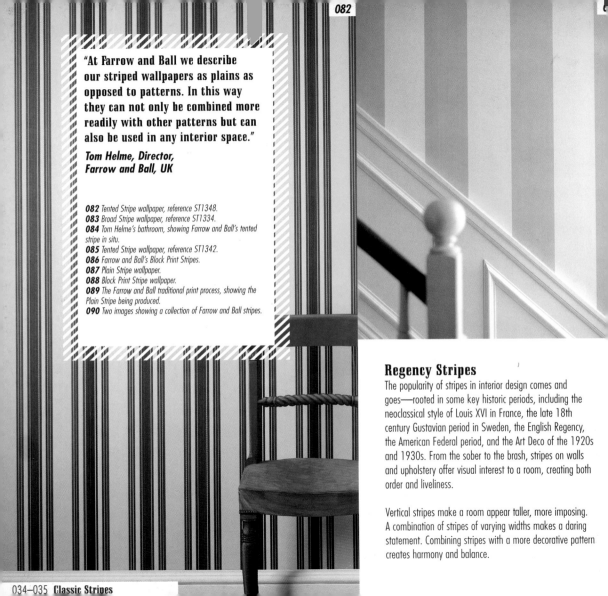

"At Farrow and Ball we describe our striped wallpapers as plains as opposed to patterns. In this way they can not only be combined more readily with other patterns but can also be used in any interior space."

*Tom Helme, Director,*
*Farrow and Ball, UK*

**082** Tented Stripe wallpaper, reference ST1348.
**083** Broad Stripe wallpaper, reference ST1334.
**084** Tom Helme's bathroom, showing Farrow and Ball's tented stripe in situ.
**085** Tented Stripe wallpaper, reference ST1342.
**086** Farrow and Ball's Block Print Stripes.
**087** Plain Stripe wallpaper.
**088** Block Print Stripe wallpaper.
**089** The Farrow and Ball traditional print process, showing the Plain Stripe being produced.
**090** Two images showing a collection of Farrow and Ball stripes.

## Regency Stripes

The popularity of stripes in interior design comes and goes—rooted in some key historic periods, including the neoclassical style of Louis XVI in France, the late 18th century Gustavian period in Sweden, the English Regency, the American Federal period, and the Art Deco of the 1920s and 1930s. From the sober to the brash, stripes on walls and upholstery offer visual interest to a room, creating both order and liveliness.

Vertical stripes make a room appear taller, more imposing. A combination of stripes of varying widths makes a daring statement. Combining stripes with a more decorative pattern creates harmony and balance.

**084**

**085**

**086**

**087**

**088**

**089**

**090**

The Regency stripe is perhaps the best known of all domestic stripes. These are even stripes of the same width in two alternating colors and were originally called "Tiger" or "Bengal" stripes. Originating in India, they were popularized by returning members of the British Raj. The Prince Regent, later George IV, was fond of them and they became a feature of the design of that period.

The tented stripe also has its origins in British history. To receive their eminent houseguest, the Duke of Wellington, returning from the Battle of Waterloo, the Bankes family decorated the attic room of their house in Devon, England, with a regimental stripe that they hoped would make him feel at home. This stripe formed the basis of Farrow and Ball's Tented Stripe wallpaper. The company still produces its papers using traditional methods. All their striped wallpapers are printed using the 19th century pan method, whereby the paper is pulled under open-bottomed troughs full of paint (not printing ink). This not only increases the depth of color, but imparts a soft chalky finish, evoking the sophistication of wallpapers from a pre-industrial age.

# Membership and Identity

Teams
School Ties and Blazers
Rank and Regiment
National Identity
Crime and Punishment
Hickory Stripes

## Membership and Identity

The fundamental ability of a stripe to distinguish or highlight something from its surroundings has meant that stripes have been used throughout history as a means of identification, signaling membership of a team, an establishment, or a country. The modern usage of stripes as an emblematic system is probably derived from their use on coats of arms—an early form of identification, essentially a means of displaying whose side you're on. Indeed, the word "stripe" can be used to describe not only membership of a physical entity but also of a category or a mindset. We talk of "being of one stripe", meaning being of one kind, sharing a set of values.

Stripes are also an important means of communicating hierarchy and rank. In sports clubs, schools, universities, and the armed forces, stripes are applied to uniforms in varying color combinations to indicate position and status—from a naval officer to a school prefect. These stripes constitute a system of merit and reward, but stripes have equally been used to segregate and punish. English and American prisoners were dressed in stripes as a means of visually distinguishing and discrediting them. Here we examine stripes that unite, identify, punish, and reward.

*091* Stripes of membership: the cap of a cub scout, with its distinctive gold stripes on green.
*092* Aeroflot's new livery designed by Identica, UK.
*093* Teams can be defined by both color and stripes.
*094* Medals on display at the ANZAC day celebrations in Sydney, Australia.
*095* Flags display stripes of national identity.
*096* Members of the same family, but different schools—brother and sister show off their school ties.

SOUTH WEST WATER

**097** A colored sash is a simple way of identifying team members.
**098** Striped ribbons identify military medals and awards.
**099** A nod to the heraldic flag in this logo for South West Water.
**100** The flag of Puerto Rico.
**101** The Hickory Stripe, once utilized on the workwear of US farmers and railroad workers.
**102** The tie of the 5th Royal Inniskilling dragoon.

093

094

095

096

097

100

101

102

## Teams

Stripes are a distinctive pattern that offer an effective way of creating standout—unifying the members of one team and making them instantly recognizable to players and fans. In the days of black and white television, stripes were particularly important in aiding viewers to identify the solid colored strip of one team against the stripes of the opponent.

Essentially, the team stripe performs a deeper function than simply that of differentiation on the pitch—this is a matter of branding. Back in 1845, the maverick I'Zingari (The Wanderers) Cricket Club designed a flag of black, red, and gold to represent the motto: "out of darkness, through fire, into light." They applied these colors to caps, blazers, and ties. From then on, sporting clubs all created their own set of colored stripes and this formed the basis of the school uniform. Signifying membership, these are emotive rather than functional stripes.

Baseball and soccer teams tend to wear vertical stripes whereas rugby teams usually wear horizontal bands. Teams can become inextricably linked to their stripes—like the New York Yankees. The Yankees first wore their distinctive pinstripe uniforms in 1912, but did not adopt the look permanently until 1915. The uniform has changed very little since then and has become one of the most famous in world sports.

**103 and 104** *Collections of vintage soccer cards show the prominence of stripes on team uniforms.*
**105** *Collectable John Player cigarette cards from 1938. The cricket series depicts players in their whites with team stripes on jumpers, blazers, and caps.*

PLAYER'S CIGARETTES

JOSEPH HARDSTAFF, JUN.

PLAYER'S CIGARETTES

W. VOCE

PLAYER'S CIGARETTES

R. W. V. ROBINS

PLAYER'S CIGARETTES

G. H. POPE

PLAYER'S CIGARETTES

F. A. WARD

PLAYER'S CIGARETTES

J. M. SIMS

RUGBY AT TWICKENHAM
BY TRAM
FROM HAMMERSMITH OR SHEPHERDS BUSH

**108**
**109**
**110**
**111**
**112**

**106** Vintage advertising, "Rugby at Twickenham" by Laura Knight, 1921. © Transport for London
**107** Girls from More House School, London, take a break from netball to model their team sashes.
**108 and 110** Football stripes: either thick single stripes or sporty multi-stripes differentiate teams.
**109** Beantown vs Amazons rugby match.
**111** All manner of sports differentiate teams with stripes—from football to polo.
**112** Supporters can pledge their allegiance to a team by wearing their own stripes.

## School Ties and Blazers

There's a paradox at work in the school tie. Its stripes, in the colors of the school uniform, are there to unify a diverse set of individuals. They say: "I belong to this establishment." Yet the tie itself is generally subjected to more customization than any other part of the school uniform. Worn back-to-front, thin end prominent, with the thick bit tucked away inside the shirt, it gives off signals of mod-ish sharpness. Tied in a thick, bulky knot with only a couple of inches of the tie's length hanging down, it says: "don't mess with me." The stripes of the establishment are therefore subverted to display membership of any number of sub-groups or simply to convey individuality.

The striped school tie and blazer was a development of the sporting colors that became popular in the mid 19th century. Students of Oxford University intertwined the ribbon bands from their boater hats to create a striped design that became the template for the modern striped necktie. By the 1920s it had become a widely used component of school uniform in England. Generally, school ties are of the more sober variety—one or two colored stripes on a dark background. Often, pupils who "win their colors" receive the honor of wearing distinctive striped ties and blazers, marking them out as high achievers.

→

## School of Boateng

**113 and 115** School of Boateng ad campaign by Peter Chadwick at Zip Design, UK , shows how the "old school tie" can take on a fashionable edge.
**114** A conflict of stripes: the tie displays conformity; worn with the sports stripes of the Fred Perry shirt, it takes on rebellious overtones.
**116 and 117** Each school is identified by stripes in varied configurations, thicknesses, and colors.

→ For the upper classes, the school tie is invested with a degree of significance that can last a lifetime. The phrase "old school tie" carries connotations of a privileged network of "old boys" recognizing a common bond, helping each other out in business or political careers. Indeed, it is possible to be defined by stripes right through one's life: from school tie, to college scarf, to career in the City— striped jackets are worn by traders on the stock exchange and pinstripes (thought to have developed from the striped club blazer) are worn by brokers and bankers alike. Thus, the stripes of membership that were often so rebelled against in school days re-emerge in later life in a parallel system of membership, signifying rank and status in the high earning business community.

**118** The origins of school uniform are in sports club ties and blazers—evidenced in this photograph from the early 20th century.

**119** The upper classes in post-war Britain maintained separate schools for boys and girls, with separate stripes to identify them.

**120** Even without the tie, the striped blazer identifies the school. More intricately striped blazers would sometimes be awarded to high achievers.

**121 and 122** Sibling rivalry: Ella and Jake sport stripy ties from their respective schools.

Week ending September 8 1956    Every Wednesday Fourpence

# JOHN BULL

123

## Rank and Regiment

Stripes form an emblematic code that indicates status, regiment, rank and merit in the military services. These stripes were developed from the heraldic system of the Middle Ages, in which stripes, chevrons, symbolic animals, and other icons were incorporated into intricate coats of arms. Simpler to reproduce, the chevron was widely adopted by the military as a recognizable symbol of honor or length of service—first appearing on French soldiers' uniforms around the late 18th century.

The British army soon followed, using these striped emblems to indicate, initially, length of service and latterly, rank: two for a corporal, three for a sergeant. The US Army and Marine Corps adopted them at around the same time, though they fluctuated between chevrons and epaulettes as rank insignia. Eventually, all the armed forces came to use stripes and chevrons in their vocabulary of rank—either pointing down (US Navy and Coast Guard) or up (US Army, Marine Corps, and Air Force). These chevrons are commonly referred to as "stripes". Because they are awarded upon promotion to a higher rank, the term "to earn one's stripes" has come to mean gaining a position through hard work and experience.

Stripes of merit are also used in medal ribbons. Endless combinations of colors are juxtaposed in differing widths so that each medal has its own set of stripes—creating a secondary identification system. Thus, members of the armed services can display their awards simply through the ribbons.

Stripes seem to have a natural affinity within the military. In the French navy, a rather more derogatory use of the stripe is employed. The common striped sailor T-shirt is worn only by members of the crew—so its blue and white stripes signify the lowest rank. Officers who make their way up through the ranks rather than passing through naval college are often referred to as "zebras," a reference to their striped shirts and their humble origins..

→

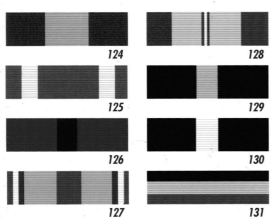

124

125

126

127

128

129

130

131

**3** Lance Corporal, Kenji Szczepanski, Marine Corps, wearing: R: Navy and Marine Corps Achievement dal, National Defence Service Medal, Service Deployment Ribbon.

**4–131** US Marine Corps form decoration:

**4** Battle of Manilla Bay (1898)
**5** Commendation
**6** Good Conduct
**7** Selected Reserve Component
**8** Combat Action Ribbon
**9** Distinguished Service
**0** Navy Cross
**1** Presidential Unit Citation
**2** Medals and decorations on display in ney, on ANZAC day, which marks the iversary of the first major military action ght by Australian and New Zealand forces ng WWI.
**3** The instantly recognizable stripes of ilor's uniform.
**4** Vintage collection of cards, depicting dals with striped ribbons.

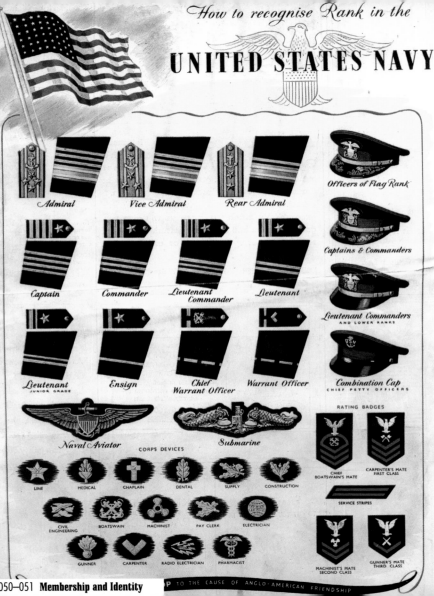

## How to recognise Rank in the

## UNITED STATES NAVY

**Admiral**  **Vice Admiral**  **Rear Admiral**  **Officers of Flag Rank**

**Captain**  **Commander**  **Lieutenant Commander**  **Lieutenant**  **Captains & Commanders**

**Lieutenant** JUNIOR GRADE  **Ensign**  **Chief Warrant Officer**  **Warrant Officer**  **Lieutenant Commanders** AND LOWER RANKS

**Combination Cap** CHIEF PETTY OFFICERS

**Naval Aviator**  **Submarine**

CORPS DEVICES

LINE  MEDICAL  CHAPLAIN  DENTAL  SUPPLY  CONSTRUCTION

CIVIL ENGINEERING  BOATSWAIN  MACHINIST  PAY CLERK  ELECTRICIAN

GUNNER  CARPENTER  RADIO ELECTRICIAN  PHARMACIST

RATING BADGES

CHIEF BOATSWAIN'S MATE  CARPENTER'S MATE FIRST CLASS

SERVICE STRIPES

MACHINIST'S MATE SECOND CLASS  GUNNER'S MATE THIRD CLASS

TO THE CAUSE OF ANGLO-AMERICAN FRIENDSHIP

**135**

**135** During WWII British newspapers ran full page explanations of how to recognize ranks in different Allied Forces.
**136** US Navy/Coastguard Rank Insignia—Seaman, E3
**137–144** US Army Rank Insignia:
**137** Private First Class (PFC)
**138** Corporal (CPL)
**139** Sergeant (SGT)
**140** Staff Sergeant (SSG)
**141** Sergeant First Class (SFC)
**142** Master Sergeant (MSG)
**143** Command Sergeant Major (CSM)
**144** First Sergeant (1SG)
**145–148** US Military Rank Insignia:
**145** Naval/Coast Guard Admiral
**146** Naval/Coast Guard Vice Admiral
**147** Naval/Coast Guard Rear Admiral (UH)
**148** Naval/Coast Guard Rear Admiral (LH)
**149** Sergeant Stripes
**150–154** US Air Force Enlisted Rank Insignia:
**150** Chief Master Sergeant (CMSGT)
**151** First Sergeant (1SGT)
**152** Command Chief Master Sergeant (CCM)
**153** Chief Master Sergeant of the Air Force (1SGT)
**154** Technical Sergeant (TSGT)

**136**

**149**

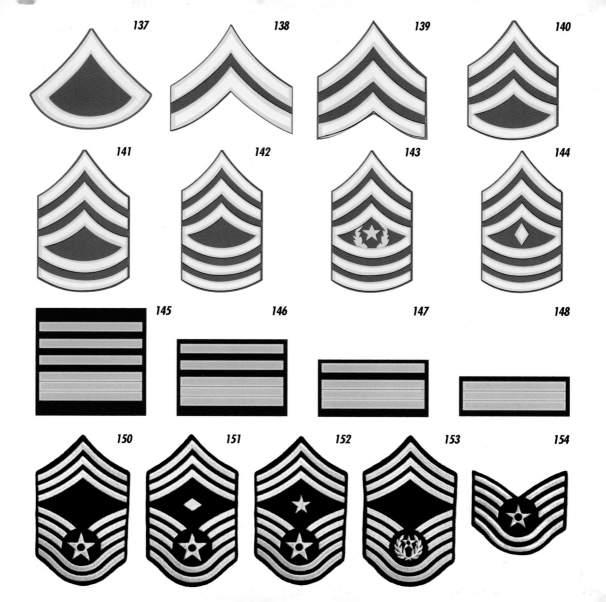

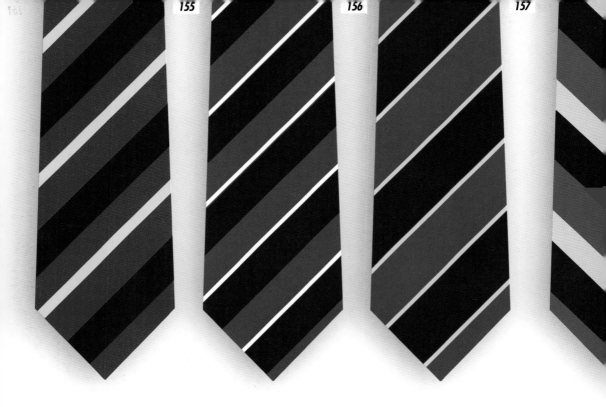

→ The British regimental tie was developed from the same system of symbolic colors used in club ties and school ties and came about at around the same time. The British army abandoned its colorful uniforms in the 1880s because they were too conspicuous in battle. Practical, low-key khaki uniforms were adopted instead, with the regimental colors transferring from uniform facings to a (usually striped) necktie. Each regiment therefore retained their colors of significance, or chose colors that would have specific symbolism.

The meanings behind the colors have, in some cases, passed into military mythology, from the patriotic: the dark blue and magenta Brigade of Guards tie is intended to represent the blue blood of the Royal Family and the red blood of the Brigade, to the heroic: the Royal Tank Corps takes its stripes from the brown mud, red blood, and green fields of Flanders.

There are strict rules on who is allowed to wear these regimental ties. Sartorial Web sites have been known to run debates about whether it is dishonorable to wear the tie of a regiment to which you don't belong. Some defend their right on the basis that they are paying honor to the regiment as long as they are aware of the history and significance of the tie. Others argue that the right to wear the tie is restricted to members of the regiment. Some British gents' outfitters will even ask for proof of regiment before they will sell the ties—ensuring that the strict system of membership and identity is adhered to.

**155** 1st King's Dragoon Guards
**156** 1st Queen's Dragoon Guards
**157** 4th/7th Royal Dragoon Guards
**158** 5th Royal Inniskilling Dragoon Guards
**159** 7th Queen's Own Hussars
**160** 8th King's Royal Irish Hussars
**161** 9th/12th Royal Lancers (POWs)

## National Identity

Countries identify themselves by a system of colors and patterns displayed on flags. Their origins can be traced back to coats of arms or ancient feudal banners—many of which used stripes. Flags constitute a global branding system: whether held aloft at cup finals, announcing the name of the local pizzeria, or planted on the surface of the moon. As the world is in a constant state of political change, new flags are always being created and old flags revived. The black, red, and gold of the German flag were replaced twice: first by Bismark and then by the Nazi party, both preferring the rather more assertive combination of black, white, and red.

It may be pure coincidence, but throughout history republics have adopted striped flags: consider the French Tricolor and the American Stars and Stripes. The origins of flags are always hard to be certain about and many revisionist theories become attached to the significance of colors. The French colors are generally accepted to represent the red and blue of the Parisian coat of arms combined with royal white to signify the reconciliation of the king with the city of Paris, but their striped configuration was probably influenced by the preceding American Revolution. These stripes had a defined purpose—set out in the 1777 Continental Congress resolution: "the flag of the thirteen United States be thirteen stripes, alternate red and white. That the union be thirteen stars, white in a blue field, representing a new constellation." Some historians also theorize that the choice of stripes was to purposefully reclaim the stripe from a symbol of oppression (prisoners of the penal colonies in Pennsylvania and Maryland wore stripes) to a symbol of liberty. Certainly, stripes have a natural affinity with libertarian movements: think of the rainbow flag—used around the world both as a symbol of peace and as the emblem of the gay rights movement. →

*162 For design purposes, a striped flag can provide a horizontal grid to house typography or information—exemplified by this use of the Dutch flag.*
*163 The heraldic nature of flags is emphasized by these woven shields—sewn on to jackets or bags, they identify the wearer as a well-travelled individual.*

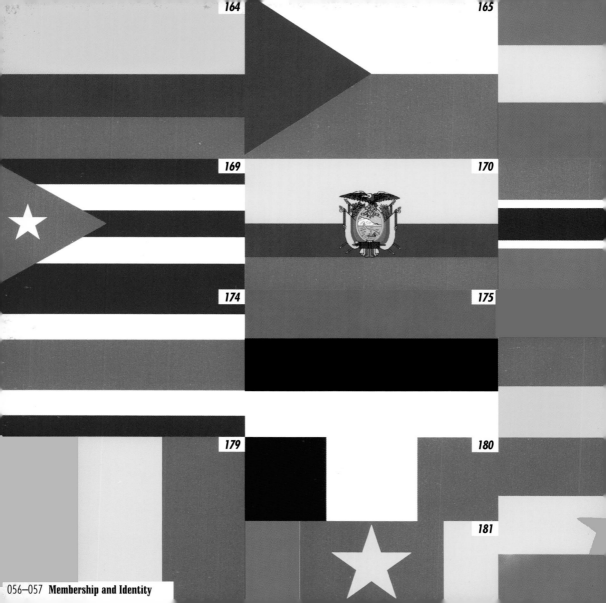

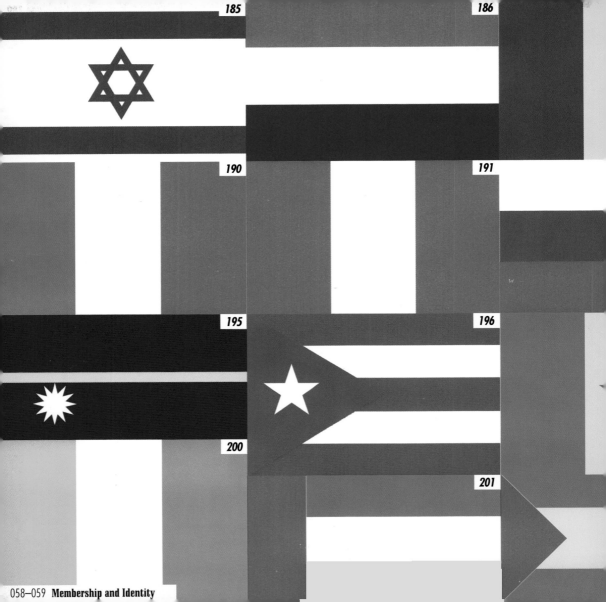

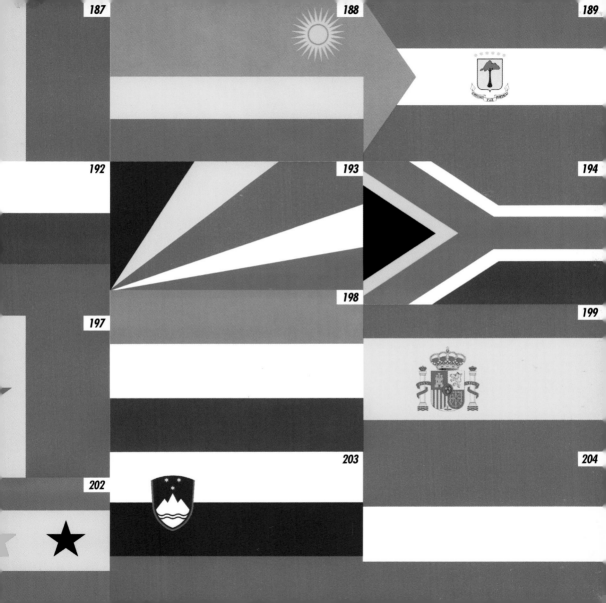

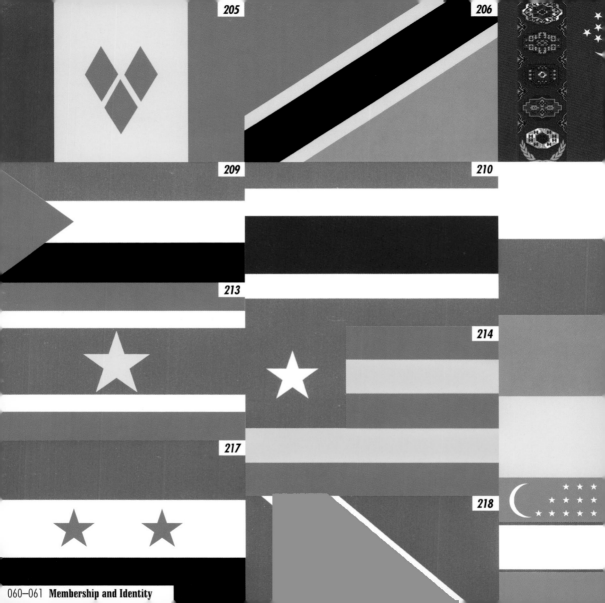

205

206

209

210

213

214

217

218

**207**

**208**

**211**

**212**

**215**

**216**

**219**

**220**

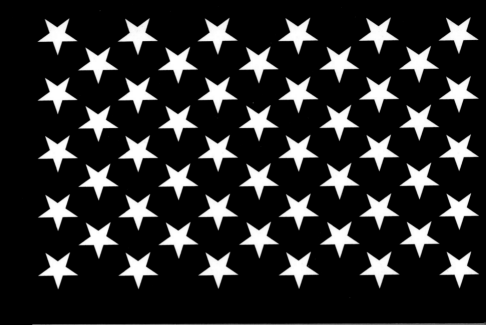

NeworderUSA

**222**

**227**

*Our future is in our hands*

**228**

LIBERTE EGALITE FRATERNITE

→ Airlines have long used their national flag as a way of distinguishing themselves. When British Airways traded in the Union Jack for a range of "world" tail fin designs, the public and press created such an outcry that the company reverted to a stylized version of the traditional Union flag. A retrogressive move, perhaps, but it certainly demonstrates the importance attached to a flag's function of demonstrating the values of a country. Perhaps this thought was uppermost when international branding consultancy, Identica, came to overhaul the Aeroflot brand.

The end of the Communist regime in 1991 saw Russia move into a new spirit of internationalism and the national airline wanted to reflect this in its identity. What better visual symbol of this than the newly reinstated Russian flag of white, blue, and red horizontal stripes, proudly emblazoned exactly where it should be—on the tail fin.

**221** Flags offer a graphic language that designers like to emulate and subvert. New Order's USA89 tour was promoted by a suitably iconoclastic Peter Saville design, based on the Stars and Stripes.
**222** State flags at the US Embassy in London.
**223** Peace flags use the symbol of freedom, the rainbow stripe.
**224** National identity isn't confined to flags—this swanky Stars and Stripes number one makes a particularly bold statement.
**225** More bold statements, this time political: the peace flag (or is it a gay rights flag?) and the Stars and Stripes with the stars replaced by corporate logos, taking a stance at an environmental rally.
**226** The Italian flag used on a restaurant's sign to guarantee authenticity.
**227** The Stars and Stripes flag made up of children's handprints—a statement of hope captured by Karol Miles.
**228** National pride displayed on this official building in France.
**229** The German flag on an army surplus coat identifies its country of origin.
**230** National flags are used by brands to appropriate the values of the country. Meta Design, Germany, designed this brand identity for German bank, Die Bundesregierung.
**231 and 232** Groups of international flags suggest unity and diversity.

224

225

226

229

230

Die
Bundesregierung

231

Salco

232

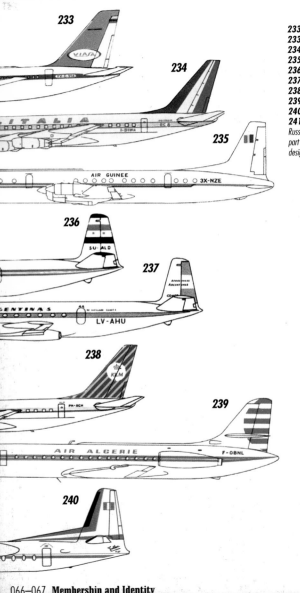

**233–240** Vintage tail fins:
**233** Viasa Venezolana Internacional de Avia
**234** Alitalia
**235** Air Guinee
**236** United Arab Airlines
**237** Aerolineas Argentinas
**238** KLM
**239** Air Algerie
**240** Nigeria Airways
**241** The red, white, and blue stripes of the Russian flag are proudly displayed on tail fins—part of the post-Soviet identity for Aeroflot, designed by UK brand consultants, Identica.

"Stripes, as well as being a dramatic visual device, can be immensely emotive especially when they reference a nation's flag. In the case of Aeroflot we used stripes on the body of the aircraft to create a modern, streamlined, contemporary look as well as on the tail fin where they promote Aeroflot as the official national flag carrier."

*Michael Peters,*
*Chairman, Identica, UK*

## Crime and Punishment

Pejorative stripes—those that degrade the wearer—have their origins in the beliefs of the Middle Ages. Then, stripes were reserved for outcasts: prostitutes, madmen, and clowns all wore stripes. Like these misfits, stripes were considered against the accepted social order. Even zebras and tigers were considered somehow demonic because of their striped coats. More recently, these distinctions have been abandoned, but in the criminal stripe, the "bad" stripe lives on. The stripe's ability to identify those who are different or dangerous was clearly behind its adoption in the 18th century penal colonies of the New World. As an identity system, stripes offer a high degree of visibility—an effective method of distinguishing between prisoner and guard, or spotting an escaped convict.

The horizontal stripes of black and white, applied in such broad widths, appear vulgar and brash—something undignified imposed on the wearer. It's no coincidence that the thick black bars also mirror the bars behind which the criminal is safely locked away from society. Stripes were chillingly adopted in Nazi concentration camps. Perhaps this ultimate abuse of human dignity was the reason for the eventual abandonment of the prisoner stripe in the West. Yet the metaphor lives on. Even now, all that is necessary to represent a criminal in a cartoon strip is to depict someone in a suit of horizontal stripes. Ironically, a similarly striped T-shirt is also the accepted way to represent a burglar—so stripes can represent both crime and punishment.

**242** Vintage Red or Dead prison stripe inspired fashion by Wayne and Gerardine Hemingway, of Hemingway Design, UK.

**243** Elvis wears prison stripes in a Jailhouse Rock promotional poster.

**244 and 245** Mark Jarrell's photographs of "The Prisoner" convention in Portmeirion, Wales, where the cult series was filmed. In the 1960s series, membership stripes were used on costumes and props to create an eerie feeling of otherness, suggesting a club you don't want to join, adding to the sense of being an outsider.

**246** Northern Sun, USA, have been designing and selling their Products for Progressives range since 1979. This striking T-shirt features a backprint that lists facts about the US prison system.

## Hickory Stripes

American railroad men wore traditional Hickory-striped bib overalls in the 19th and early 20th centuries and they became a sort of uniform for the railroads. Different gangs of workers would have worn overalls woven and manufactured by different companies, and so each workforce probably wore varying stripes. One of the largest producers of such overalls was Key Industries, who still produce a version of them. Hickory cloth was also used for uniforms in the American Civil war. New Yorkers heading west to the Californian gold fields wore shirts made from it.

The term "Hick", meaning a rural dweller lacking urban sophistication, is linked to Hickory stripes, though it is unclear where the true connection lies. The fabric might have been so called because, much like denim, it displayed the strength of hickory wood. Or it might have derived its name from the fact that it was produced specifically for workers, and therefore people of a lower social class. They had already been given this derisive name—taken from the hickory canes with which less progressive rural schoolteachers used to punish their pupils. Whatever the origin, the Hickory stripe continues to be synonymous with workwear garments, linked to a tradition of hard work and simple values.

*247 - 266 Modern design often takes its inspiration from the past. These 21st century denims are based on archive Hickory striped fabric used in US workwear from the turn of the 20th century.*

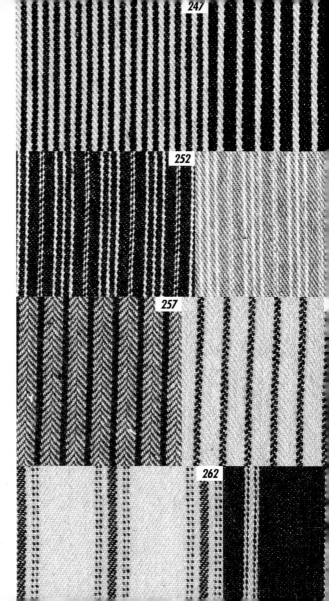

# Themes and Moods

Elegance
Fun
Nautical
Natural
Sport
Speed

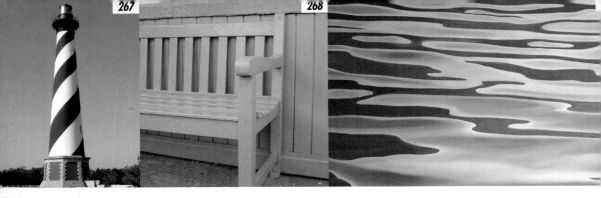

## Themes and Moods

According to popular psychology, seeing stripes in your dreams suggests that you are making a bold and daring statement. Horizontal stripes mean you're straightforward; vertical stripes are non-conformist. Dream of black and white vertical stripes and you might be confronting your close-minded side. It's impossible to evaluate the accuracy of these interpretations—they simply serve to highlight the complex nature of stripes. With endless permutations of color, proportion, and direction, the stripe possesses the ability to communicate a whole range of ideas and emotions.

Designers manipulate stripes to convey elegance, fun, and speed. They can be brash, youthful, sporty, and nautical. Stripes can have an organic, natural appearance, or create a moody, urban atmosphere. Brands like Paul Smith and Adidas have made stripes their signature, yet these are very different businesses, selling different types of product. The versatility of stripes means that they can both own a different type of stripe—elegant on the one hand, sporty on the other. With such a variety of adjectives applicable to the stripe, this section groups stripes into the most common themes they communicate and the moods they evoke.

**267–269** *A selection of stripes that create a nautical mood.*
**270** *Sporty stripes applied to a netball.*
**271** *Stripes inspired by nature: Lucienne Day's 1961 print, Larch.*
**272** *The elegant stripes of the onion towers on St Basil's Cathedral, Red Square, Moscow.*
**273** *The fun stripes of kite tails inspired this illustration by Rob Hare.*
**274 and 275** *Speed stripes created by streaks of light.*
**276** *A jolly striped teapot to brighten up breakfast.*

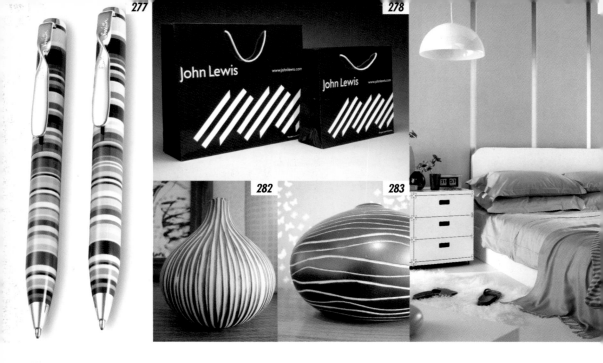

## Elegance

The stripe treads a fine line between the brash and the subtle. Too broad a stripe and it becomes clumsy. Too much contrast between the colors and it becomes a hazard sign. How do you ensure your stripes will be elegant? There's no set formula for coming up with a refined stripe. It's very much down to the subtlety of the design process—another aspect of the complexity of communicating with stripes. Proportion is key to creating an elegant effect. Decorators use striped papers and fabrics to visually heighten a room, making its proportions appear more opulent. Fashion designers use the stripe in similar ways: pinstripes can elongate the look of a sleek suit; shirting stripes give a smart, fresh finish. The spacing of the stripes is crucial to the end result. When a pinstripe turns into a thicker chalk stripe, the suit moves from elegant to showy.

Subtlety of color and lightness of touch play a big part. Tone-on-tone stripes in a restricted color palette will produce an elegant effect because the eye reads the overall pattern as a harmonious block rather than an interrupted surface. Delicately etched lines on glass, wood, or metal create random striations rather than formal stripes. Again, these feel elegant and sophisticated. Inspired by LA sunrises, Visopia's Eos Light Pillars create an elegant mood because their many strips of colored light softly merge and fade into one another, always in a state of transition, never static and harsh.

Even multicolored stripes can be elegant. Take the signature stripes of fashion designer, Paul Smith. Surely such a random design should produce something garish? Not in his skillful hands. The unexpected color juxtapositions, the fine proportions, and the confident application of these stripes, whether woven in cotton shirting or applied to fine china and finished with a gold band, all exudes contemporary elegance.  →

**277** Write elegant prose with these striped Paul Smith pens.
**278** Stripes exude understated elegance in the revamped John Lewis Partnership identity by John McConnell, with design assistants, Andrew Ross and Laura Coley, Pentagram, UK.
**279** Dulux, UK, creates a stylish, feminine interior using a clean, vertical, metallic stripe.
**280** Paul Smith's signature striped tableware takes on a sophisticated air with the addition of a delicate gilt edge.

**281** In her recent collection for Comfort Station, UK, Amy Anderson creates elegant and bold accessories with a strong graphic element, such as this tan handbag with its daring black stripes.
**282 and 283** Etched ceramic and wood vases are lent an elegant quality by the delicate striations that create a warm texture and a natural feel.

"Inspired by the sunrises of LA and named after Eos, the mythical goddess of dawn, Visopia's Light Pillars shift colors before your eyes. Moving and pulsing, its color stripes effuse a light-hearted sophistication, bathing an environment with both rich and subtle luminescent hues."

*Ronny Bagdadi,*
*Visopia, USA*

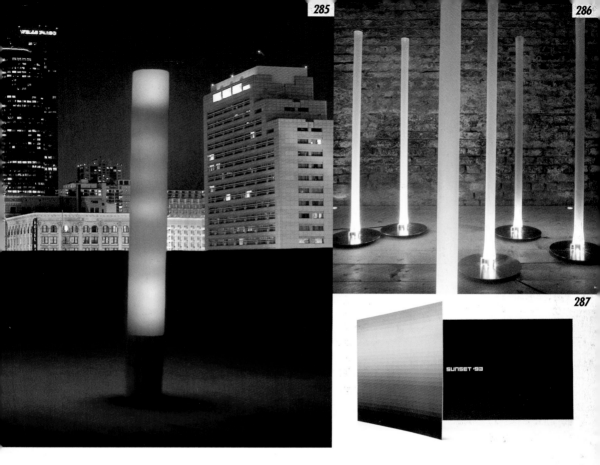

**284 and 285** *The Eos light by Visopia, US, is a remote controlled freestanding light that emits a varying luminescent stripe, allowing you to alternate between different interior moods. Based on the sunrises of LA, the merging and blending colored light brings hotel glamor into the home.*

**286** *The DidjLIGHT is an award-winning light with a dual purpose—it's a light and a musical instrument. Developed by Triebholz, Germany, it's a glass didgeridoo, which can be played in the same way as its eucalyptus antipodean ancestor.*
**287** *More stripes of light: Sunset 93 Sunrise 94, Yohji Yamamoto New Year Card. Art Direction by Peter Saville, design by Brett Wickens.*

"The Paul Smith way started innocently and came about because of my love of craftsmanship, tradition, Britishness, but also my love of humor. Because of this, 'classic with a twist' was born and now it is a very over-used phrase, but still very relevant today.

My most famous logo is the multicolored stripe originally used for a shirt but now used for many things, including our packaging and shop carrier bags—this was created in the early 1980s. If you can imagine, when I designed my first collection in 1976, it was quite difficult to find many interesting fabrics for men, especially for shirts; they were all very classical and the quantity I could order was very small so it was impossible to create exclusive ideas for me. So by the early 1980s I had used every combination of stripes, but at last I was in a position to design my own exclusive fabrics. With this in mind, I decided to create the 'definitive stripe' using many, many colors—this was an immediate success and has continued to be my signature."

*Sir Paul Smith,*
*Paul Smith*

289

292

293

Metallic stripes create a sense of opulence, exemplified by the timeless packaging for Yves Saint Laurent's Rive Gauche perfume. An icon since its launch in 1968, there's more than a little Parisian sophistication here. In shiny silver and glossy blue or black, it ought to look brash (even a little gauche?) but somehow its uncompromising confidence oozes style.

**289** Delicate white stripes enhance the elegant form of these glass vessels by Daniel Wooddell.
**290** One of a series of striped catalog covers for Brits Design, Imago en Identiteit, Peter Saville Associates, UK.
**291** Enduring 1960s elegance: Rive Gauche's stripes transferred effortlessly to the more recently launched men's fragrance range.
**292** Exotic stripes create an Eastern mood.
**293** St Basil's is a Moscow must-see: elegant, exotic, and enchanting.
**294** Rimmington Vian's softly retro vases combine sugared almond interiors with elegantly etched exterior stripes.

**295**

**296**

**299**

**301**

**302**

**303**

## Fun stripes

Memories of childhood vacations spent by the seaside conjure up myriad multicolored stripes in bright primaries and soft pastels. So many fun things associated with the seaside are striped—think of deck chairs, helter skelters, swim shorts, beach huts, seaside candy rock, parasols, and windbreakers.

Childhood itself is also filled with striped things—candy, clothes, and toys are all frequently striped. While striped adult clothes can suggest a gauche desire to shock, children's clothes in stripes simply look cheerful and innocently exuberant.

Multicolored stripes can offer exciting color combinations and lively, eye-catching pattern that is youthful and dynamic. Thick, bold stripes of red on yellow or white are bright and cheerful, with a celebratory mood that makes us think of circus big tops. Striped candy canes have a festive spirit that reminds us of the holiday season.

Designers often use stripes as a short hand for fun. Add multicolored stripes to a logo and you create a kids' range. Cover a simple chair in brightly striated fabric and it becomes relaxed, even humorous. Add stripes to toothpaste and suddenly, even brushing your teeth becomes fun!

**295** A cheery beach cabana from The Conran Shop, UK.
**296** Roll up, roll up! A stripy Big Top spells excitement.
**297** Signal pioneered the striped toothpaste that makes brushing fun.
**298** Vintage swim shorts in seaside stripes.
**299** The August chair by Alexander Taylor, UK, covered in Maharam's Miller stripe fabric from Kvadrat.
**300** Multicolored stripes have a natural affinity with childhood.
**301–303** Helter skelters and candy are stripy seaside treats.
**304** Fun storage: Droog straps used in an interior scheme by The Apartment, US.

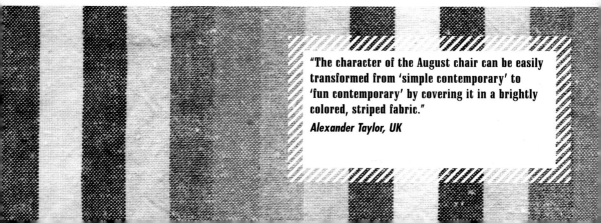

"The character of the August chair can be easily transformed from 'simple contemporary' to 'fun contemporary' by covering it in a brightly colored, striped fabric."
*Alexander Taylor, UK*

305
306
311

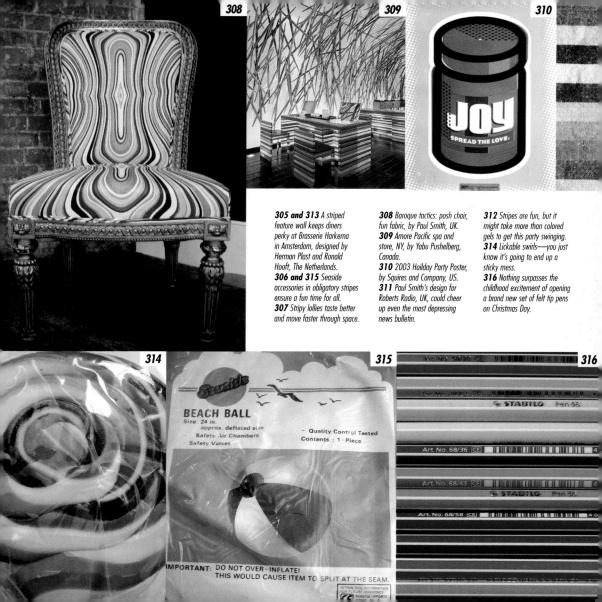

**305 and 313** A striped feature wall keeps diners perky at Brasserie Harkema in Amsterdam, designed by Herman Plast and Ronald Hooft, The Netherlands.
**306 and 315** Seaside accessories in obligatory stripes ensure a fun time for all.
**307** Stripy lollies taste better and move faster through space.

**308** Baroque tactics: posh chair, fun fabric, by Paul Smith, UK.
**309** Amore Pacific spa and store, NY, by Yabu Pushelberg, Canada.
**310** 2003 Hoilday Party Poster, by Squires and Company, US.
**311** Paul Smith's design for Roberts Radio, UK, could cheer up even the most depressing news bulletin.

**312** Stripes are fun, but it might take more than colored gels to get this party swinging.
**314** Lickable swirls—you just know it's going to end up a sticky mess.
**316** Nothing surpasses the childhood excitement of opening a brand new set of felt tip pens on Christmas Day.

popcorn

317

318

**POP CORN**

322

321

325

324

**317** Vintage popcorn carton.
**318** Colorful gloves brighten up a winter beach trip.
**319** Find a space: a sea of umbrellas by the sea.
**320** The sculptural forms of B&B Italia's UP5 and UP6 represent a female form chained to a ball, signifying the "shackles that keep women subjugated." Designed by Gaetano Pesce in 1969, its serious message is lightened with striped beige and orange jersey fabric.

**321** The multicolored stripes on the 2.4 chair by Omer Arbel, US, are formed by sandwiching the colors between clear resin.
**322** Wheeeeee!
**323** Exciting stripes of smoke from the tails of formation airplanes.
**324 and 325** No denying that stripy candy is full of fun.
**326** The striped soft top of the Citroën 2CV Dolly clearly designates this car as a pleasure-mobile.

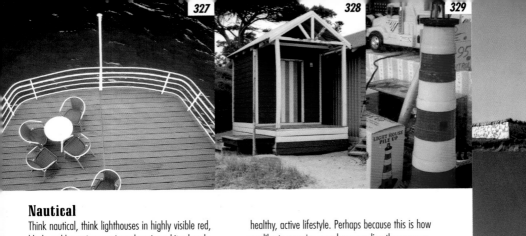

## Nautical

Think nautical, think lighthouses in highly visible red, black, or blue stripes against gleaming white; beach huts, smartly painted in sea blues and sandy creams; ship-shape decks of scrubbed down timber and jaunty sailor tops in navy and white. While the seaside promenade is lined with multicolored fun stripes, nautical stripes represent the stage before the stripe reaches the shore. They are more closely associated with sailors, ships, naval crew, and the sea itself.

Nautical stripes are simple yet smart. Navy blue and white are the classics. They suggest fresh air and a healthy, active lifestyle. Perhaps because this is how we like to perceive ourselves spending the summer months, many a summer fashion collection includes a take on the nautical theme—and inevitably, stripes figure. Since we first started flocking to the seaside for vacations in the mid-19th century, we have appropriated the stripes of fishermen and sailors and worn them for active daywear and dapper evening attire.    →

*327–331, 333, and 335–338* Nautical stripes are to be found on beach huts, lighthouses, and decking, predominantly blue and white. *332 and 334* The lighthouse and its stripes became the obvious choice for the smart Lands' End identity designed by DJ Stout and Julie Savasky, Pentagram, US.

334

Lands' En
**MEN'S JEANS**

SIZE 30W 34L
COLOR INDIGO
STYLE # 84760
CONTENT 100% COTTON

COUNTRY OF ORIGIN Made in
Dominican Republic of U.S. Fabric
SKU # 1426275

"Lands' End was founded by a professional sailor who originally published a mail-order catalog offering sailing tack and equipment. As it evolved into an apparel catalog, their nautical history has remained an important part of the company's heritage. The idea of a lighthouse for their icon seemed like a natural, as it is a highly visible beacon that marks the place where the land meets the sea, or 'The Land's End'. The distinctive stripes that adorn lighthouses were introduced as an identity pattern that could be used as an additional tool for expressing the Lands' End brand."

*DJ Stout, Pentagram, US*

ANDS'END
DIRECT MERCHANTS

338

LANDS END

LANDS END

LANDS END

→ Many nautical elements are naturally striped. The grooves of a wooden boardwalk, stretching out towards an expanse of rippled sand and wavy sea beyond fills the eye with stripes and curves. The color palette ranges from soft aqua through to deep ultramarine. Even the horizon of sand, sea, and sky can be abstracted to striped bands of color.

We can't resist bringing this fresh and clean look into our homes. Tongue and groove cladding, painted in various shades of blue, teamed with bleached timber flooring and accessorized with a plethora of shells and starfish seems to mirror the serene beauty of the nautical environment. It creates a domestic oasis of calm, a year-round summer vacation without leaving the house.

**339** Holkham beach, Norfolk, UK: the vast seaside horizon can form the most impressive nautical stripe.
**340** Seafront shelter in uniform blue.
**341** The nautical influence on this tongue and groove bathroom by Fired Earth, UK, is clear.
**342 and 343** Boardwalks of stripy decking make a dip in the sea irresistible.

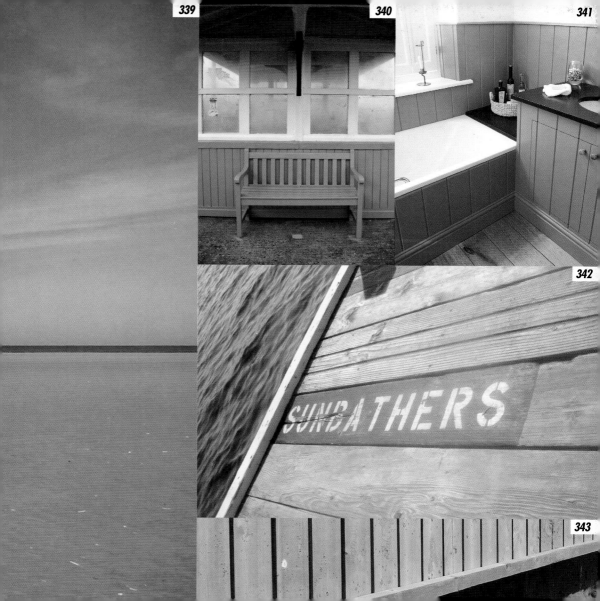

339
340
341
342
SUNBATHERS
343

**344**

**345**

**344, 345, 347, and 348** The contours of rippled sand are constantly changing nautical stripes, recreated every time the tide changes.

**346 and 355** Beach decking, in strips of sun bleached wood, offer bare feet a welcome relief from baking hot sand.

**349** A sandpiper picks its way across a beach of rippled sand in this evocative design for accessories by Camp Apparel, US.

**348**

**349**

**354**

**346**

**347**

**351**

**352**

**353**

**357**

**356**

**350** The ridges of a seashell are nautical stripes that you can take home with you as a souvenir.
**351** Complete the shabby chic, nautical look with a distressed paint finish in classic seaside blue on wooden panelled doors.
**352, 356, and 357** More striped horizons of sand, sea, and sky. The color palette moves from sandy beige through aquamarine to sky blue.
**353** Quick: still a few sun loungers left! A man-made jetty stretches out into the Mediterranean Sea, offering Italian sunworshipers reclaimed space.
**354** Gentle waves create more ripples—another striped motif that complements the rippled sand.

**358** The photo-realistic ripples of this "Wave" mural by Natura Design Solutions, US, creates an atmosphere of calm and relaxation.

**359** This "Tsunami" textile print by Marimekko, Finland, suggests movement by using stripes and curves in a dramatic way. The colorway is the height of nautical chic.

**360** This boldly striped interior by Dulux, UK, also plays with movement in a calmer, but no less graphic way.

## Natural

Richard Of York Gave Battle In Vain. This simple mnemonic is learnt in childhood to memorize the seven colors of the rainbow. When white light is refracted by drops of water in the atmosphere it separates into its component colors, creating stripes of pure colored light, always in the same sequence: Red, Orange, Yellow, Green, Blue, Indigo, and Violet. To see a rainbow in the sky is uplifting and fills us with optimism. Rainbows are naturally occurring stripes whose colors have come to represent peace, harmony, and freedom.

*361, 362, 365, and 367* Flowers are prized for their natural stripes.
*363, 364, and 368* In search of a pot of gold: the rainbow represents peace, harmony, and freedom—themes explored in Rob Hare's illustration.
*366* A beautifully sun-streaked sky tops a layer of fog.

Natural stripes have been prized throughout history, with flowers cultivated specifically to produce variegations in their coloring. In 17th century Holland, striped tulips were so fashionable that a single bulb could change hands for the equivalent of four times an average worker's annual salary. There was a stripe pecking order too: red-on-white were the most prized, fetching substantially more than purple-on-white or yellow-on-red stripes. Unbeknown to Holland's horticultural speculators, they were paying handsomely for diseased stock—the striated petals were actually the result of a virus attacking the bulb. →

363

364

366

368

**372** **373** **374** **377** **378** **380**

RITHMA
MUSIC FICTION

**369–376** Foliage can be striped in an amazing array of colors, offering vibrancy in the absence of flowers. The veins of large tropical leaves create natural stripes that are particularly prominent when backlit by the sun.

**377** Abstracting natural stripes can lead to exotic results, seen here in the atmospheric night scene on this album sleeve by Red Design, UK.

**378–380** Grasses, wild flowers, and trees all create dynamic stripes in the natural environment—whether gently swaying or still and statuesque.

**381–383** The majestic pencil straight birch tree is the subject of this series of custom-designed, hand-painted murals by Natura Design Solutions, US. "Birch" and "Winter Birch" are seen here in detail and in situ, the latter making a stunning backdrop of graphic stripes, the perfect complement to 1950s inspired furniture.

**384 and 385** "Deers in the Forest" wallpaper by Absolute Zero° offers a modern, natural twist on the Regency stripe.

**386** Inspiring environment: vertical stripes formed by a forest of trees.

**387 and 388** Forest stripes captured in an illustrative style on promotional banners by spacecadet design, Canada, for Motherbrand's "Cabin" project.

384

385

387

388

"Natura's images are representational but rooted in modernism...Barnett Newman, Mondrian, and Giacometti. The natural striped compositions are designed to be integrated into the architecture and relate to the vertical harmony of a space, as well as a standing figure or figures. The illusion of atmospheric depth pushes and pulls in a way that adds movement to an interior."

*Jason Gaillard,*
*Natura Design Solutions, US*

→ There are stripes everywhere in nature: look at the delicate veins of a palm leaf, the rugged grooves of tree bark, the orange tips of the red hot poker plant. A forest of pencil straight birch trees creates an environment of irregular vertical stripes—the view through the trees randomly broken up by slender trunks. Birch trees hold a particular allure for architects, designers, and artists. They provide an organic foil for stark minimalist architecture. Their fine proportions and delicate coloring abstract into a beautiful striped configuration that is skillfully recreated in Jason Gaillard's handpainted murals.

The structure of plants and trees has been a great influence on the textiles of British designer, Lucienne Day. Her "Sequoia" print, designed in 1959 for London furniture store, Heal's, uses large-scale graphic stripes of black on block color. Intended for use as a single long drop, the bold design was inspired by the giant redwoods that grow in the forests of California.

**389 and 390** *Details of stripy bark.*
**391** *Lucienne Day's "Sequoia" print was part of a series of 1950s textiles with an arboreal theme, intended to create a large-scale, architectural feel.*

## Sport

Stripes are intrinsic to the format and rules of sport. From football pitch to tennis court, athletic track to rugby ground, stripes define the field of play, one's allotted lane, what's in play, and what's out of touch. We spectate from the touchline and cheer at the finishing line.

The sports stripe encompasses both the stripes that are applied within the sports arena and the emblematic stripes that are worn as part of a team's kit. The dominant color palette is bold and simple: white, green, and black dominate, with flashes of primary red, blue, and yellow.

Modern sports kit has developed from the club stripes of the 19th century, when cricket clubs and rowing clubs first started to adopt striped blazers, ties, and sweaters. These stripes are bold enough to distinguish one team from another. They also display allegiance—just as an army regimental tie or a striped national flag shows which side you're on.

Lance Wyman's celebrated logo for the Mexico City 1968 Olympics is considered a seminal piece of sporting graphic design. Its concentric black stripes and curves are based on traditional Mexican art and culture, but also seem to reference the oval of an athletic track. It developed into an op art black and white striped visual identity that was applied to everything from signage to memorabilia.　→

**392 and 393**
*Kyle E. Chambers, US, shot these amazing track and field photographs. Stunningly graphic, they also serve to highlight the functional importance of stripes in the sports arena.*

ROCHESTER
ROCHESTER
ROCHESTER

**394**

**398**

Make Brit

**400**

**394** Stripes keep athletes on the right track.
**395** A stack of hurdles creates another sporty stripe.
**396** The combination of material, form, and color, not to mention the application of bold asymmetric stripes, lend an unequivocally sporty edge to the 8.0 chair by Omer Arbel at Some, Canada.
**397–399** More sports stripes in white, yellow, and blue, marking boundaries and fields of play.
**400** Even couch potatoes can convey a sporty air with the simple addition of a stripy sweat band.
**401** London's successful Olympic 2012 bid was supported by a striped motif that charts the flow of the River Thames.

**402** *The referee's black and white stripes clearly differentia[te] him from the players on the football pitch.*

**403, 405, and 406** *Hard [to] beat: Lance Wyman's identity [for] the 1968 Mexico City Olympi[cs is] a piece of sports design histo[ry]. It incorporates the Olympic rin[gs,] ancient Mexican art, and a hi[nt] of the running track.*

**404** *The three stripes of Adi[das] are one of sport's best recog[nized] symbols. For the 21st century, Adidas has rationalized its br[and] into three distinct lines. Sport Performance offers functional[,] innovative sports products. Sp[ort] Heritage concentrates on tren[d] setting streetwear. Sport Styl[e] shapes the future of sportswe[ar] for the fashion conscious.*

**407**

**410**

→ Arguably the most famous sports stripe is the one that comes in threes: the three stripes of Adidas, part of the brand since Adi Dassler first used them on a pair of shoes in 1949. The stripes originated from a functional necessity—Dassler used them as a means of providing support to the side of the shoe. An astute businessman, he quickly registered the stripes as a trademark of Adidas. Over the decades, they have helped Adidas become one of the world's most recognizable brands.

→

**412**

"The three stripes are inextricably linked to the Adidas brand. When introducing Adidas to China, such brand elements were paramount, because they create both credibility and prestige. Chinese customers know the three stripes are a mark of quality, and at the same time they look cool—that intangible feature that all discerning customers seek. As Official Sportswear Partner of the Beijing 2008 Olympic Games, Adidas is looking forward to cementing its relationship with Chinese consumers."

**Sandrine Zerbib**
*Head of Adidas, Greater China*

Olympic Gold winner, Roman
shows off all the shoes he wore
pete in the decathlon.
he Tokio 64. When launched for
cyo Olympics in 1964 it was the
 track shoe ever made.
avid Beckham scores by
n Bridge.
he adiStar High Jump, as worn
trie Cloete at the 2004 Athens
cs, has the South African flag
dered on the back of the shoe.

**411** *The Allyson Felix adiStar Demolisher.*
**412** *Greek weightlifter, Pyrros Dymas, wins a bronze.*
**413** *The most colorful of personalized shoes—Maurice Greene's adiStar DeMOlisher II features a flow of stripes and stars.*
**414** *The PredatorPulse II Dragon— part of David Beckham's exclusive range.*

**415–418 and 422–424**
Adidas Sport Heritage constantly reinvents classic styles to create fresh streetwear, as seen in these collections from F/W 2004 and S/S 2005.

**419** Retro styling gives personality to this 2003 ad for The Rekord—part of the Adidas Originals range.
**420** To mark the 35th anniversary of the launch of the classic Adidas Superstar, a range of 35 customized shoes were created by artists and celebrities. Shown here is the Ian Brown Superstar.
**421** The Superstar Adi Dassler celebrates the man who started it all.

→ The three stripes first appeared on sweatsuits in 1962, creating an iconic piece of sportswear that represents the very essence of sport itself. In 197? the trefoil logo was introduced, building on the significance of threes. The three leaves symbolized the three continental plates of the world, portrayin Adidas as a uniting force in sport.

Today's Adidas is a carefully managed business with three (that number again) divisions: Sport Performance, Sport Heritage, and Sport Style. Each division has its own design ethos and products, targeted to different audiences, united by the three stripes.

**420**

EVERY  HAS A STORY

**The Rekord**

Other shoes may have dominated centre court. But no one could touch these bad boys when it came to PE class. Check out the Rekord, in six authentic colour combinations, at adidas.com/originals.

FROM A TIME WHEN YOUR DAD
HAD THIN SOLES AND THICK HAIR.

422

423

424

425

426

431

430

## Speed

Blurring, merging, distorting stripes of light that seem to whiz past the viewer create the effect of speed. These glowing lines, captured by a long photographic exposure, are the ghosts of headlights and rear lights of speeding vehicles, long gone. Too fast to hang around, speed stripes represent what is no longer there. Think of Roadrunner: cartoonists create the suggestion of speed through blurred stripes, whizzing behind the character.

Remember when cars were emblazoned down the side with go-faster stripes? These questionable add-ons were a must-have in the 1970s— a decade of cop shows and TV car chases. The third star of *Starsky and Hutch* was undoubtedly their red car with its broad white stripe tapering to a point at the front and running across the roof at the rear. This was a decade when it was paramount to convey the attitude of speed, even if your car did a maximum of 65mph. As long as it looked fast, it was cool.

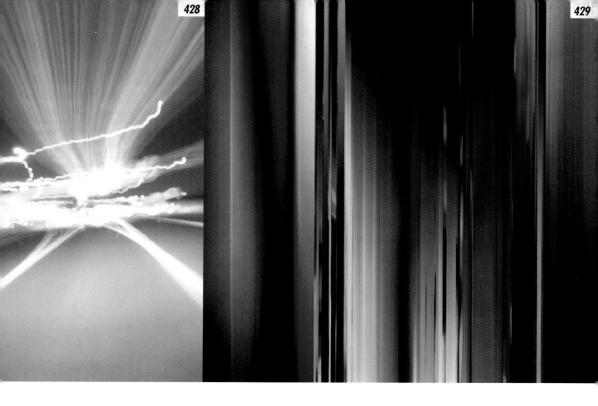

These days, cars really do go fast—they just don't shout about it. Ironically, the speed stripe is now more likely to be found on a mobile home than a car. But motorboats, buses, and trains all continue the tradition of the speed stripe. With its aerodynamic striped "E" logo that combines dynamism and style, the Eurostar train confirms its status as the speediest and most stylish route between London and Paris.

**425–428 and 430–432** *Speeding through the city at night: photographers capture the sense of speed with blurring streaks of light in highly evocative images that are shorthand for fast, urban life.*
**429** *Waste painting # 1, 1998, by Paul Hetherington, Peter Saville, and Howard Wakefield. Collection Emmanuel de Buretel. The blurring and merging of strips of color creates dynamic movement.*

433

434

436

437

439

440

**433–441** Popular in the 1970s, surely due for a comeback: a selection of surviving go-faster stripes on cars, trucks, mobile homes, buses, and boats.
**442** Speed and elegance come together in the streamlined logo for the Eurostar train service, by Minale Tattersfield, UK.
**443** Launched in 1994, the Eurostar service made history as the first passenger service to go direct (via the Channel Tunnel) from London to Paris, Lille, or Brussels.

# Signals and Information

## Signals and Information

Stripes crop up on food packaging, maps, and rulers, helping us to choose the right flavor, take the quickest route, or measure a window. Stripes hold digital information, like bar codes; they act as a visual guide, like the color bars of a television test card; they convey information in a recognized format, like the routes and directions on a map.

Designers use stripes to turn the volume up. In advertising terms they "create standout"; they draw attention to things. That's why they're painted on the backs of ambulances, across restricted areas, and on posts. Yellow and black stripes warn us that the bee stings. Disruptive stripes create confusion between what the eye sees and what the brain perceives, creating optical illusions. Similar visual chaos helps camouflage zebras, tigers, and even battleships.

In everyday life, stripes convey codes and signals that differentiate, so we can make informed choices about color, flavor, and zone. We buy the right shampoo for our hair type by recognizing the colored strip on the packaging. We put a letter in a striped envelope to differentiate between overland mail and airmail. Throughout history, the barber, the butcher, and the grocer have displayed stripes outside their establishments to differentiate themselves on the high street.

These are the stripes you will find on everyday signage and products. Pay homage in this section to the stripe as signifier, differentiator, and indicator. Take another look at the stripe that disguises and the stripe that conceals, the stripe that highlights and the stripe that reveals.

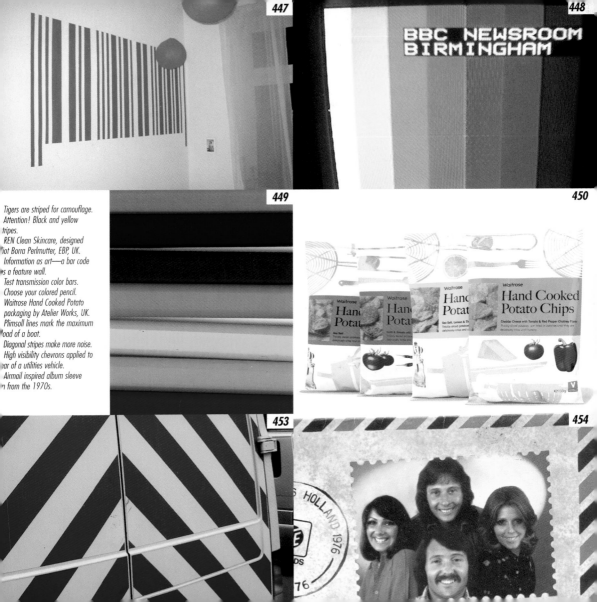

447

448

BBC NEWSROOM BIRMINGHAM

449

450

Tigers are striped for camouflage.
Attention! Black and yellow
stripes.
REN Clean Skincare, designed
by Borra Perlmutter, EBP, UK.
Information as art—a bar code
as a feature wall.
Test transmission color bars.
Choose your colored pencil.
Waitrose Hand Cooked Potato
packaging by Atelier Works, UK.
Plimsoll lines mark the maximum
load of a boat.
Diagonal stripes make more noise.
High visibility chevrons applied to
rear of a utilities vehicle.
Airmail inspired album sleeve
from the 1970s.

453

454

## Signaling Flags

In maritime communication, stripes overcome language barriers. The system of codes developed over many years of maritime history, with varying symbols used by each country until the early 20th century. Now standardized into the International Code of Maritime Signals, each flag represents a letter and each pennant represents a number. Used to convey messages from ship to ship, or from ship to shore, some of the flags employ circles and crosses, but many of them use stripes to convey meaning.

For swift communication of standard messages, each flag has a secondary meaning. So you might use the yellow and blue striped flag to represent the letter K within a specific word, or you could display it to say: "You should stop your vessel instantly." Watch out for the diagonal yellow and red stripes of the O flag—it means: "Man overboard."

Boats, water, and light inspire American artist, Luke J. Tornatzky. His depiction of signaling flags flying from the tall mast of a ship has the air of a triumphant homecoming—bright, optimistic, and uplifting. Such is the nautical appeal of these graphically patterned, colorful flags that they are often to be found strewn across the facades of buildings in ports and seaside towns for pure decoration, belying their essential communication function.

*456 Isolated striped flags from the International Code of Maritime Signals—watch out for the O!*
*456 A seafood restaurant adorns the entrance passageway with signal flags to create the impression of a fresh catch.*
*457 "Coming Home" by Luke J. Tornatzky, USA.*
*458 A 1960s windcheater jacket label creates a nautical feel by spelling out the brand name, "Mighty Mac" in the symbols of the International Code of Maritime Signals.*

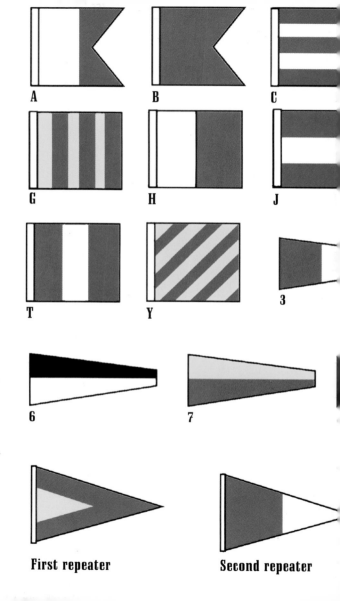

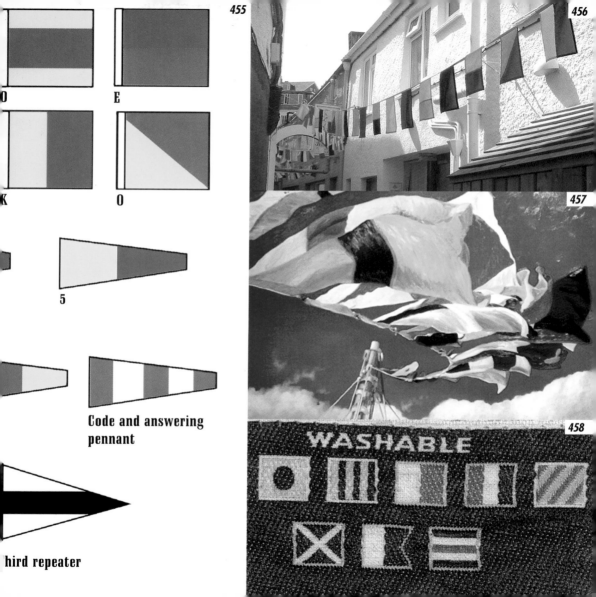

455

456

457

**D**

**E**

**K**

**O**

**5**

Code and answering pennant

Third repeater

458

WASHABLE

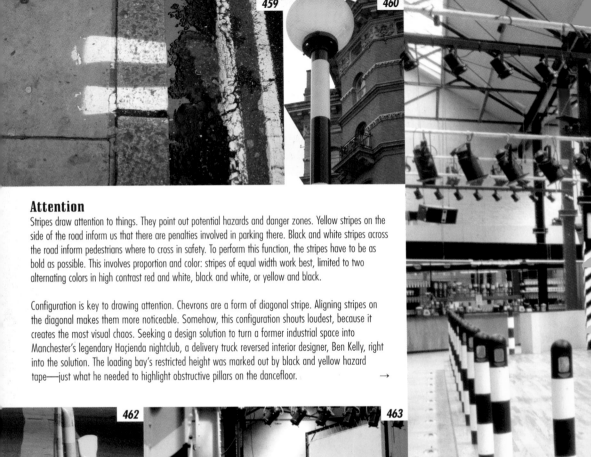

## Attention

Stripes draw attention to things. They point out potential hazards and danger zones. Yellow stripes on the side of the road inform us that there are penalties involved in parking there. Black and white stripes across the road inform pedestrians where to cross in safety. To perform this function, the stripes have to be as bold as possible. This involves proportion and color: stripes of equal width work best, limited to two alternating colors in high contrast red and white, black and white, or yellow and black.

Configuration is key to drawing attention. Chevrons are a form of diagonal stripe. Aligning stripes on the diagonal makes them more noticeable. Somehow, this configuration shouts loudest, because it creates the most visual chaos. Seeking a design solution to turn a former industrial space into Manchester's legendary Haçienda nightclub, a delivery truck reversed interior designer, Ben Kelly, right into the solution. The loading bay's restricted height was marked out by black and yellow hazard tape—just what he needed to highlight obstructive pillars on the dancefloor. →

"Creating a nightclub out of an industrial space, we had genuine safety issues to consider, such as changes in level and obstructive pillars on the dance floor. I wanted to retain the integrity of the space and it just seemed natural to use the language of hazard signs, already part of most industrial environments. The yellow and black chevron tape and roadside posts did a practical job, but also created a visual style for the club. Peter Saville developed the stripes and chevrons from the 3-D space into 2-D graphic devices that created a strong, unified identity for the club."

*Ben Kelly, UK*

*459, 460, and 462* Stripes in the urban environment can highlight hazards, signal warning, and communicate information.
*461 and 463* The iconic Haçienda interior by Ben Kelly Design, UK.

**464**

**465**

**471**

**472**

**473**

USE HEARING PROTECTION

MAY 19-THE DURUTTI COLUMN/JILTED JOHN

MAY 26-BIG IN JAPAN/MANICURED NOISE

# THE FACTORY

JUNE 2-THE DURUTTI COLUMN/CABARET VO

JUNE 9-THE TILLER BOYS/JOY DIVISION

**RUSSEL CLUB ROYCE RD MOSS SIDE**

HALFORDS

## High Security Steering Wheel Bar

Meets British Insurance Industry's Criteria for
Vehicle Security – Category 3

HAÇIENDA

→ It was the start of a visual language for the club that has influenced interior and graphic designers for over two decades. Even if he wanted to escape stripes, Kelly's clients seek him out to revive them, with enticements like: "Wouldn't it be great to do a Haçienda for kids?"—the brief to design The Basement at London's Science Museum. Again, when design consultants Lippa Pearce were commissioned to work with car accessory store, Halfords, a happy union was formed with Ben Kelly Design, and yellow and black stripes became a key element of the new visual identity. →

**464** Subway platform—stay behind the yellow line for safety.
**465** Fire truck, UK.
**466** Promotional poster from 1978 Factory event, Peter Saville, UK.
**467** Decommissioned sea mine.
**468** The Fernsehturm is Berlin's tallest structure.
**469** Red and white stripes are a common warning on land or at sea.
**470** No stopping on a UK red route.
**471** Black and yellow road barriers.
**472** UK police car.
**473** Attention-grabbing aquatic stripes.
**474** Halfords packaging designed by Lippa Pearce, UK.
**475** Haçienda first anniversary celebration poster by Peter Saville, UK.
**476** Power station, Moscow.
**477** Stripes guide loading vehicles.
**478** Scaffolding is striped for visibility.

**479, 480, 482, and 483** Exterior and interior shots of car accessories retailer, Halfords. The branding and retail design concept was a collaboration between Lippa Pearce, UK, and Ben Kelly Design, UK. Stripes and chevrons are used as a bold device that creates an industrial feel and, significantly, directs customers to retail zones, information desks, service bays, entrance, and exit.

**481** Yellow diagonal stripes mark out sections of a train platform that are designated "Keep Clear" areas—a vital part of the traffic management system.

→ Russia is in a state of economic transition. The urban landscape is cluttered with advertising messages trying to reach the affluent new middle class. One brand wishing to cut through the clutter, mobile telecommunications operator Beeline, approached international branding consultancy Wolff Olins, for a smart, simple solution. The fussy image of a bee was dropped in favor of the bee's most attention-grabbing attributes—its stripes.

enjoy

whatever you're into

билайн

486    487

«Бизнес-формул...»
Тарифные решения
оптимальное для каждого сотрудника и комп...

«Максима...»
Идеальный вариант для тех,
...объять весь мир

«БУМ»
Оптимальный вариант для тех,
кто любит говорить долго

«Тайм»

"Beeline, the Russian mobile company, had a heritage and a history. Based on the image of the bumblebee, it had great recognition. Our brief was to graphically retain some of that heritage.

Wolff Olins created a brand identity that is about imagination. It uses the black and yellow stripes rather than the actual image of a bumblebee. We created a language—the world of Beeline—in which the stripes take you wherever you want to go."

**Marina Willer, Creative Director, Wolff Olins, UK**

**484 and 485** From ice creams to alarm clocks, any object can borrow the distinctive black and yellow bee stripes in Wolff Ollins' bold identity system for the Russian mobile telecommunications brand, Beeline.
**486–488** Stripes of inspiration: industrious bees show off their stripes as they go about their work, captured in these glorious shots by Christine Jamieson.

**489**

**490**

**494**

**495**

## Camouflage

According to folk legend, the tiger's black stripes are the marks of retribution, made by burning rope after he was tied up and set alight by the farmer whose "wisdom" he tried to steal. The zebra was once considered a diabolical creature as a result of its striped coat, which was seen as a transgression against the laws of nature.

The reality is that zebras and tigers are striped as a means of camouflage. We commonly think of camouflage as a technique used by creatures to mimic their natural surroundings, blending in to avoid detection by predators. Stripes are too distinctive to blend in; the tiger and zebra use them to create confusion. The zebra employs what is known as "disruptive" camouflage. Its stripes help to break up the edges of its silhouette, so it's less easy to make out by its chief predator, the color-blind lion. Tigers go one step further. Their stripes are disruptive but their main body coloring also blends in to the background of long grasses. Combining both "disruptive" and "blending", camouflage is termed "coincident disruption". The same principle is employed in modern military camouflage. →

**491**

**492**

**493**

**496**

The tiger combines blending and disruptive camouflage ... stripes and background color.

**... and 491** Pete Ark's pictures show the zebra's disruptive ..., which help it avoid becoming lunch and also earned it the ...ation for being "the most elegantly dressed" animal.

**..., 493, and 496** Zebras feature in the LAVADA project by ...er, Crystal Barlow, US. The concept is for a boutique and ...nizable clothing line that uses the idea of camouflage in ...e. The consumer gets to choose the scale and style of ... by means of projecting it onto white garments.

... Animal prints like tiger and zebra are often used in interiors ...ate an exotic mood.

... Ride the Tiger identity by EBP, UK, for a streamed online ...venture.

**... and 498** Identica, UK, used a zebra concealed among ...s in the striking packaging for the Copyguard brand they ...d. Themes of protection and camouflage were particularly ...nt to the product—a film that protects documents from ...horized photocopy and faxing.

**497**

**498**

™

COPYGUARD

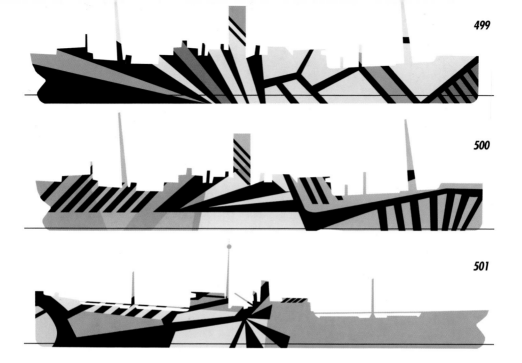

*499*

*500*

*501*

*502*

→ Disruptive camouflage achieved its ultimate application with the creation of "dazzle" camouflage during WWI. The British marine painter, Lieutenant-Commander Norman Wilkinson had the idea of painting battle ships with bold diagonal stripes and zig-zags. They became known as "dazzle ships". The patterns broke up the ship's outline and shape, confusing the German U-boat gunner as to the target's course and speed, because when he tried to piece together the two halves displayed in the optics of the rangefinder, the pattern didn't seem to fit.

4,400 ships received the dazzle treatment—half of them under the supervision of Vorticist painter, Edward Wadsworth, who recorded the process in his own paintings. While the effectiveness of dazzle painting was never proven, the practice continued until the end of WWII. Meanwhile, dazzle patterns became a public craze, applied to everything from swimsuits to trucks.

→

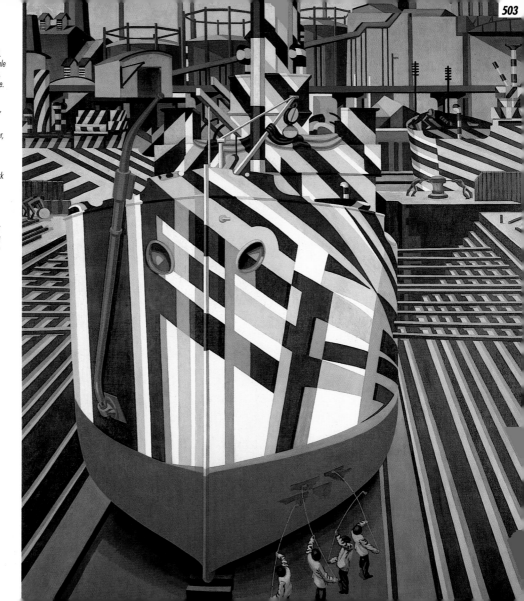

**9–501** Razzle dazzle
~es: various dazzle
~ouflage designs from WWI.
~ designs were tested on scale
~els, rotated on a turntable,
~ viewed through a periscope.
~tive designs were then
~missioned under the
~rvision of "dazzle officers"
~ as Edward Wadsworth.
~ The Dutch paddle steamer,
~and, in 1916, painted in
~le camouflage and in use
~ hospital ship.
~ "Dazzle Ships In Dry Dock
~verpool," 1919, painted
~orticist painter, Edward
~sworth, as his official war
~mission while he was
~seeing the painting of over
~0 such ships. The painting
~hangs in the National
~ry of Canada.

**506**

→ The rooms at The Standard, Downtown LA, have an ingenious design feature, reminiscent of dazzle camouflage. A bold graphic stripe is applied to walls, curtains, and light fittings, harmonizing all the interior fixtures, and creating an arresting visual effect that blurs the boundaries between textile, interior, and graphic design.

*504–506 The Standard, Downtown LA, has rooms with graphics by art director, Shawn Hausman, produced by Nancy Nielsen.*

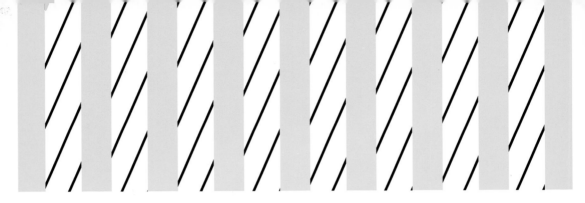

## Optical Effects

Stripes can be deceivers. They figure in a great number of optical illusions—whereby the human visual system is fooled into perceiving something that isn't there or incorrectly perceiving what is there. The brain adds to the information it receives from the eye, relying on a number of in-built assumptions to make sense of the raw data. In an optical illusion, these assumptions are misdirected. Many optical illusions distort our perception of size, length, or curvature. Striped optical illusions create warped perspective and color deception. They make straight lines appear curved and static images appear to be in motion.

This phenomenon is key to the works of artists of the 1960s op art movement. Concerned with surface kinetics, many of the works were produced in high contrast black and white and create the visual effect of movement: they appear to pulsate, vibrate, swell, and warp. The term "op art" was coined in a 1964 edition of *TIME* magazine, though these techniques had been explored in works such as Victor Vasarely's "Zebra" (1938). In 1965 the New York show, "The Responsive Eye," at the Museum of Modern Art introduced op art into the public consciousness. →

**507 and 508** *This optical illusion shows how overlaying diagonal stripes with bold vertical ones tricks the brain into believing that the diagonals don't line up. Below are the diagonal stripes without the vertical ones—where it becomes apparent that they do indeed line up.*
**509** *Known as the "café wall" illusion, this optical effect comes from observing staggered tiles on the wall of a café. The alternate colored tiles give the illusion of the horizontal plains converging when in fact they run parallel.*

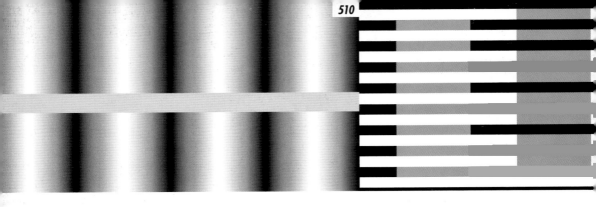

**510** Because of the shading on the background vertical stripes, the horizontal flat gray stripe seems to be modulated.

**511** Both blocks of green are the same color but the horizontal black stripes placed behind and in front of the colors make the green block with the black stripes placed behind seem darker.

**512** This three-color striped pattern gives the impression of using four due to the closely placed colors having an effect on each other. Next to magenta, the green takes on a blue hue and reads as a fourth color—turquoise. Next to the orange it has a purer green hue.

**513** Stare at the center of this flag for at least 30 seconds. Then look at a piece of white paper or a white wall. You'll see a true representation of the colors of the American flag.

**514–516** Dianne Calgaro knitted this alien scarf from Debbie Stoller's Stitch'n'Bitch Handbook. The alien face appears in the rib when viewed from a different angle.

The cover of the show's catalog featured the work of Bridget Riley, considered the leading exponent of op art. Graduating from London's Royal College of Art in 1955, she became interested in the pointillist works of Seurat. From 1961 to 1965 she produced a large body of abstract work that used black and white geometric shapes—predominantly stripes—to create amazing optical effects. Other artists linked to op art include Carlos Cruz-Diez, Adolf Fleischmann, Daniel Buren, and Jesus Rafael Soto.

Op art had a huge influence on fashion and graphic design of the 1960s. Such is the relationship between the world of art and commerce that it quickly moved into the broader cultural arena. Bridget Riley in particular fought against this, attempting to sue an American company for basing a fabric design on one of her paintings. There's no denying the lasting influence of op art. Today we can still witness its effect on advertising, design, and fashion. Perhaps its perceived accessibility is key to its perennial application. Linked to our fascination with optical illusions, we enjoy interacting with the works. We marvel at the way they use simple elements, like the stripe, to create complex works that raise questions about perception and reality. Or perhaps we just enjoy witnessing our brains being fooled into seeing something that we know cannot be real. →

512

514

515

516

**517** This illusion relies on the brain interpreting converging stripes as perspective, so that the chair on the right looks bigger than that on the left. In fact, all the chairs are the same size.

**518** These stripes of gray, though completely flat color, seem to be darker on the left edge where they meet a lighter color.

**519** Here the converging lines seem to bend the straight vertical stripes.

**520** These stripes create a 3-D, raised effect by altering in width. Again the brain assumes that the lines are communicating perspective.

**521–523 and 525** Retail outlet, Comfort Station, UK, utilizes optical effects on its floor to create an arresting visual experience and give a greater sense of space.

**524** NB:Studio, UK, used op art references in their design for corporate brand consultancy Merchant's 2002 handbook.

"Having limited floor space in my boutique meant that I had to be clever designing the interior to feel bigger, using linear optical illusion techniques to create a sense of movement, space, and excitement."
*Amy Anderson, Comfort Station, UK*

526

528

529

527

→ Stripes can distort reality to our benefit. Just as wearing horizontal stripes creates the illusion of a broader physique, applying unconventional horizontal stripes to an interior can create the illusion of space, even in rooms of modest proportions. In the design scheme of The Birchin, a warehouse conversion where the apartments are purposefully compact to ensure affordability, Hemingway Design used horizontal striped wallpaper to create a sense of space and drama—a bold application of stripes that appeals on both functional and esthetic levels.

*526–530 The broad stripes of this wallpaper by Hemingway Design, UK, can create the illusion of making a room seem taller when hung vertically or wider used horizontally.*

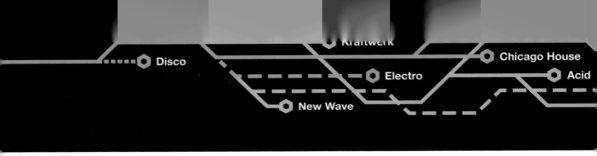

Disco   Kraftwerk   Electro   Chicago House   New Wave   Acid

## Routes and Directions

You know where you are with stripes. Literally. Striped lines form the basis of most of the world's railway and underground maps. Take the London Underground; its map is a design classic. Designed in 1933 by electrical draughtsman, Harry Beck, its triumph was to stray from strict geographic representation, visually reducing the system to a simple design, based on the circuit diagrams he drew for his day job.

The map's colors and shapes are synonymous with London. It is applied to all manner of tourist memorabilia, from hats to tea towels. Recently, a design-led merchandising initiative, All Zones, has given innovative product designers the chance to create contemporary furnishings and accessories using elements of London Transport's design heritage.

Inevitably, the Tube map features prominently in many of the young designers' contributions. The circular station interchange symbol becomes a holding device for the numerals of a stripy clock face; the individual colored lines are magnified to create graphic ceramic tile designs. Abstracted and isolated, the colors of the Tube lines become decorative, geometric, and fun. The color juxtapositions seem odd, yet familiar. The stripes (all taken from one source) range from hi-tech crisp to psychedelic opulent.                                              →

**531, 539, and 547** *Title sequence to the TV series "Pump up the Volume," about the history of house music. Designed by Zip Design, UK.*
**532** *Transforming the everyday into a gift. This photo-etched stainless steel map of the London Underground credit card sized. © Transport for London designed by SUCK UK.*
**533** *The current London map is faithful to the Harry Beck original. © Transport for London.*
**534–538** *Abstract decorative tiles, celebrating the intersection of tube lines, by Art Meets Matter, UK, for the All Zones project. © Transport for London designed by Art Meets Matter.*

534

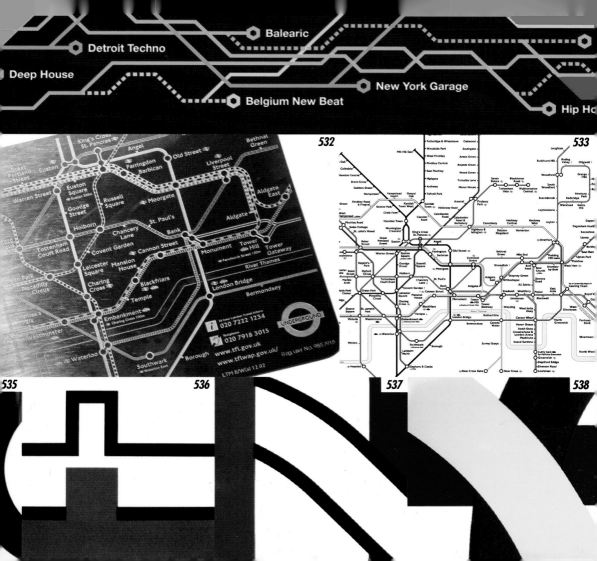

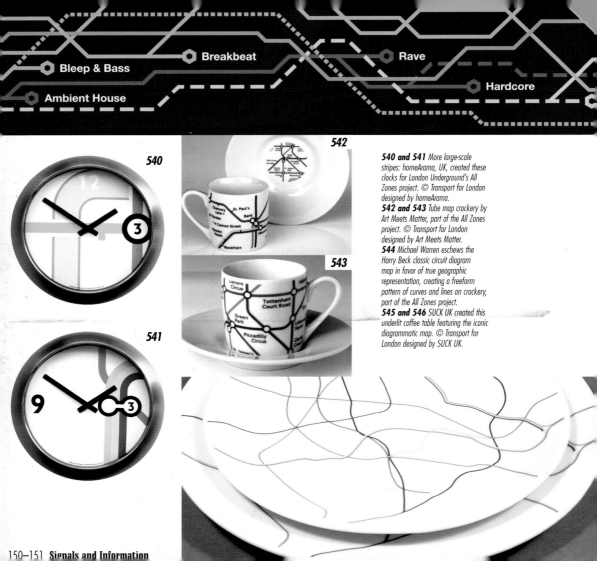

Bleep & Bass

Ambient House

Breakbeat

Rave

Hardcore

**540**

**541**

**542**

**543**

**540 and 541** More large-scale stripes: homeArama, UK, created these clocks for London Underground's All Zones project. © Transport for London designed by homeArama.

**542 and 543** Tube map crockery by Art Meets Matter, part of the All Zones project. © Transport for London designed by Art Meets Matter.

**544** Michael Warren eschews the Harry Beck classic circuit diagram map in favor of true geographic representation, creating a freeform pattern of curves and lines on crockery, part of the All Zones project.

**545 and 546** SUCK UK created this underlit coffee table featuring the iconic diagrammatic map. © Transport for London designed by SUCK UK.

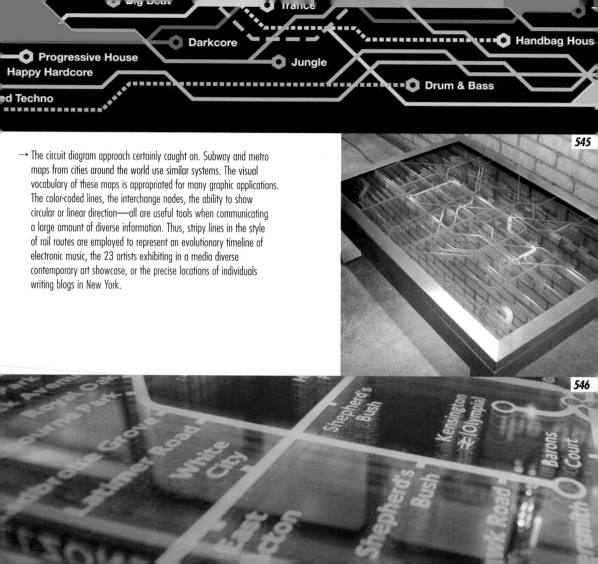

Darkcore  Handbag House

Progressive House  Jungle

Happy Hardcore  Drum & Bass

ed Techno

→ The circuit diagram approach certainly caught on. Subway and metro maps from cities around the world use similar systems. The visual vocabulary of these maps is appropriated for many graphic applications. The color-coded lines, the interchange nodes, the ability to show circular or linear direction—all are useful tools when communicating a large amount of diverse information. Thus, stripy lines in the style of rail routes are employed to represent an evolutionary timeline of electronic music, the 23 artists exhibiting in a media diverse contemporary art showcase, or the precise locations of individuals writing blogs in New York.

545

546

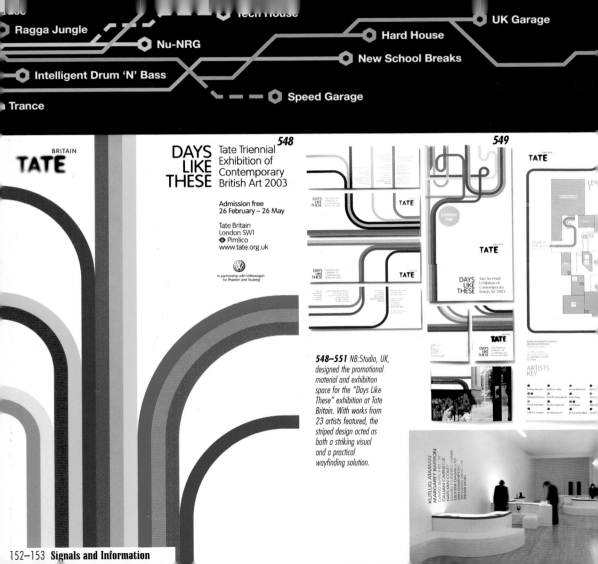

Ragga Jungle

Nu-NRG

Tech House

Hard House

UK Garage

New School Breaks

Intelligent Drum 'N' Bass

Speed Garage

Trance

BRITAIN
TATE

**DAYS LIKE THESE** Tate Triennial Exhibition of Contemporary British Art 2003

**548**

Admission free
26 February – 26 May

Tate Britain
London SW1
⊖ Pimlico
www.tate.org.uk

In partnership with Volkswagen
for Phaeton and Touareg

**549**

*548–551* NB:Studio, UK, designed the promotional material and exhibition space for the "Days Like These" exhibition at Tate Britain. With works from 23 artists featured, the striped design acted as both a striking visual and a practical wayfinding solution.

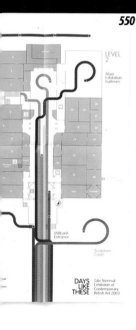

**550**

**552**

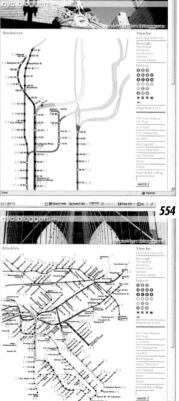

**553**

**554**

**552–554** The NYC Bloggers Web site shows bloggers, categorized by area and the subway stop closest to them, creating a geographic plan of New York's online activity.

## Bar codes

In the often-striped language of commerce and retail, the bar code is surely the most stripy and yet the most inscrutable. Unless you're a computer. They are striped for a reason; each stripe represents a number in a 12-digit code, holding information about the country of origin, the manufacturer, and a product code. Like striped tattoos, each one unique, bar codes represent the DNA of a product.

When bar codes were first introduced, they were hidden away. Purely functional, they were considered a necessary evil—unsightly distractions from the purity of any packaging concept. As designers and artists increasingly find beauty in the everyday and mundane, bar codes have become a source of creative inspiration. As a graphic language,

they have the advantage of immediately communicating themes of technology and commerce. Create a stars and stripes flag out of a bar code and you make a satirical comment on Western consumerism.

Some designers embrace the bar code as a graphic element in its own right—like the CD cover from Norwegian designer, Rune Mortensen. Here the bar code becomes an integral part of the design—the typography works in harmony with the bar code, which occupies a prominent position. The Red Snapper CD cover by UK designers, Non-Format, mixes imagery of fashion and retail—making the bar code prominent and teaming it with an individually stitched label.     →

**555**

**556**

**557**

**558**

Frozen by
Blizzard Winds

Kevin Drumm
Lasse Marhaug

**559**

SLAVE

**560**

CAT NO:     LCD35

ARTIST/TITLE:  RED SNAPPER / RED SNAPPER

TRACKS:  10     DATE: 2003

BARCODE: 6 66017 05242 7     HTTP://WWW.LORECORDINGS.COM

03 ]   0000000000000  LCD   35  MADE IN ENGLAND

DESIGN: NON-FORMAT.COM

red
snapper
A LO QUALITY PRODUCT

[ ...RADISE REMIX]

TRACK: TITLE:

01   REGRETTABLE
02   MOUNTAINS AND VALLEYS
03   ULTRAVIOLET
04   HEAVY PETTING
05   DNIPRO

Ⓟ LO RECORDINGS 2003     Ⓒ ...S 2003

THIS SNAPPER LP IS A COLLECTION OF UNRELEASED MATERIAL,
LIVE TRACKS AND REMIXES OF AND BY THE TRIO. DUE TO THE
DEMISE OF NUPHONIC RECORDS THIS YEAR THE FINAL SNAPPER EP
NEVER HAD A RELEASE. RICH, DAVID AND ALI FELT THAT THEY
OWED IT TO THEIR FANS TO GET THIS AND OTHER MATERIAL
RELEASED AND THEY ARE GRATEFUL TO LO RECORDINGS FOR
BELIEVING AND MAKING IT POSSIBLE.

THIS MUSIC IS DEDICATED ... E PEOPLE WHO HAVE WORKED
WITH US AND SUPPORTED US SIN... 994

**555** Björn Ehlert took this image of
the bar coded stage curtain, a suitably
commerce-related design by Bente
Lykke Møller for the Royal Dramatic
Theatre in Stockholm's production of
the "The Merchant of Venice."
**556** The bar code stripes make a
stylish graphic statement on this sofa
by Swedese, Sweden.
**557** The bar code is proudly
displayed on the cover of "Frozen by
Blizzard Winds," designed by Rune
Mortensen, Norway.
**558** Red Snapper CD cover by
Non-Format, UK.
**559** Bar codes can be used to make
a big statement: "Slave" tattoo by
Scott Blake, US.
**560** Scott Blake, US, pictured in
front of a collection of his bar code art.

**561** *Scott Blake, US, uses bar codes to create detailed portraits of celebrities like Elvis. Stand back and appreciate it.*

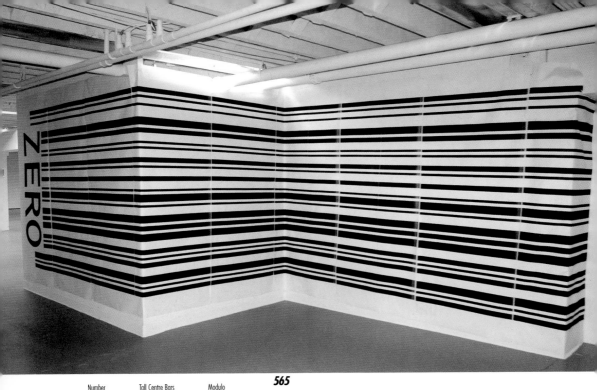

565

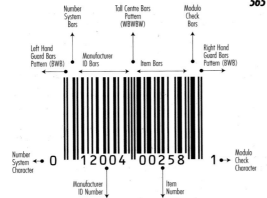

Number System Bars

Tall Centre Bars Pattern (WBWBW)

Modulo Check Bars

Left Hand Guard Bars Pattern (BWB)

Manufacturer ID Bars

Item Bars

Right Hand Guard Bars Pattern (BWB)

Number System Character

0   12004   00258   1

Modulo Check Character

Manufacturer ID Number

Item Number

72410 31286

→ Scott Blake's art is entirely created from bar codes. On his celebrated Web site, barcodeart.com, he describes his art as being about "downloading data from the Internet and remixing to make something I can call my own." To create the works he pixelates iconic images and replaces the pixels with individual bar codes. Because each bar code has different proportions of black stripe to white space, each has a different "grayscale value." When combined, they have the effect of a monochromatic mosaic. His art thrives on popular culture: "I cut bar codes from my brother's music CDs, ex-wife's cosmetics, and roommate's book collection. I bar code anything and everything. Faces, time, tattoos, graffiti, drugs, and even mouse clicks. Bar codes are labels on life. In a way, my bar code art works backwards, by creating life from those labels."

**562 and 564** More artwork by Scott Blake, whose Web site includes details of how to bar code yourself.
**563** Illustrator Wojtek Kozak creates a comment on consumerism representing the Stars and Stripes flag as a bar code.
**565** Scott Blake has a great "science" section on his site that explains the workings of bar codes and we thank him for enlightening us with this explanation. This standard UPC A code works as follows: Left Hand Guard Bars: These stripes are a "start" reference for the barcode scanner. Number System

Character: This numeral identifies a type of manufacturer or how the code is to be used. For example, 0 is usually assigned to the retail industry, along with 6 and 7. Number System Bars: These stripes correspond to the above. Manufacturer ID Number: The Uniform Code Council assigns each company a personal six digit ID number to be used on all their products, composed of a Number System Character, and a five digit code. Manufacturer ID Bars: These stripes relate to the Manufacturer ID Number. Tall Center Bar: A middle reference point for the scanner. Item Number: Manufacturers assign

these unique five digit codes to each of their products. Item Bars: These stripes correspond to the above. Modulo Check Character: This is a numeral derived from a formula based on the unique set of numbers in each code which helps ensure the accuracy of the scan. Modulo Check Bars: These correspond to the above. Right Hand Guard Bars: An ending reference point for the scanner.
**566** Bars and Stripes software enables the user to create their own bar codes on a PC. Based in the US, their identity says it all.

## Commerce

The red and white stripes of the barber's pole have gruesome origins. They go back to the days when barbers acted as surgeon and dentist as well as offering hair cutting and shaving. Bloodletting (thought to prevent or rid disease) was a particularly common service. Bloody bandages would be washed and left outside the shop to dry—blowing in the wind and wrapping around the shop's pole, creating the familiar spiral effect. It is thought that the white stripe symbolizes the bandage and the red stripe, the bloody arm of the patient.

Striped awnings above shops hark back to a simpler time. In the days before main street shopping was replaced by a weekly trip to the superstore, striped awnings would herald the wares of each individual trader: red and white for the butcher, green and white for the grocer. Once inside the shop, stripes would be repeated on aprons, hats, and paper bags. The butcher's blue and white apron is a guarantee of hygienic premises and reliable service. These days, sole traders wishing to convey a sense of nostalgia still use stripes—you'll find them outside old-fashioned confectioners and antique shops.

Aware of the reassuring nature of these commercial stripes, UK supermarket chain, Tesco, incorporates the stripes of a grocer's awning into its logo. This lends the brand an element of down to earth trustworthiness. They're saying: "we're just like your local grocer—only a bit bigger."

**570**

**571**

**572**

**575**

**576**

**577**

**580**

**581**

**567, 568, and 573** The jaunty stripes of the barber's pole belie its grisly origins of blood and bandages.

**569** UK retailer, Tesco, conveys main street values with its grocer's stripes.

**570, 571, and 574–581** The striped awning harks back to a simpler commercial heritage. Today it evokes good old-fashioned values and suggests retail with a personal touch.

**572** Spic and span stripes guarantee fish fried in hygienic surroundings.

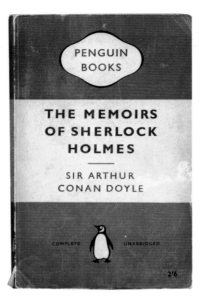

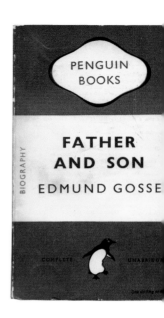

162–163 Signals and Information

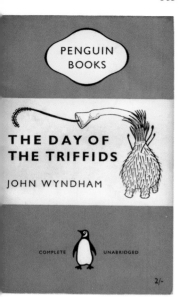

## Differentiation

Stripes can be extremely helpful in ensuring you're on the right floor, or you've chosen the correct flavor soup. We're talking stripes of differentiation. These are the colored bands on books, paint tubes, and store directories that help indicate range, color, and zone.

The first Penguin books were launched using the horizontal grid designed in 1935 by Edward Young. The range was split into a number of themes, each with its own distinctive color—applied to the covers as two bold striped bands that house the Penguin branding. Title information is uniformly positioned in a white central band. The range included blue for biography, green for crime, and the enduring orange for fiction—perhaps the only lasting element of the original design, now a key feature of Penguin's brand. Updated in 1948 by Jan Tschichold, the horizontal grid lasted well into the 1950s.  →

*582–585 A selection of Penguin paperbacks, illustrating clearly how Edward Young's horizontal grid helped differentiate between subject matter. The format was so successful that it lasted nearly a quarter of a century. **586 and 587** The packaging for 4th_Floor hair products, designed by North, UK, uses varying widths of stripe in different colors to indicate the right product for your hair type.*

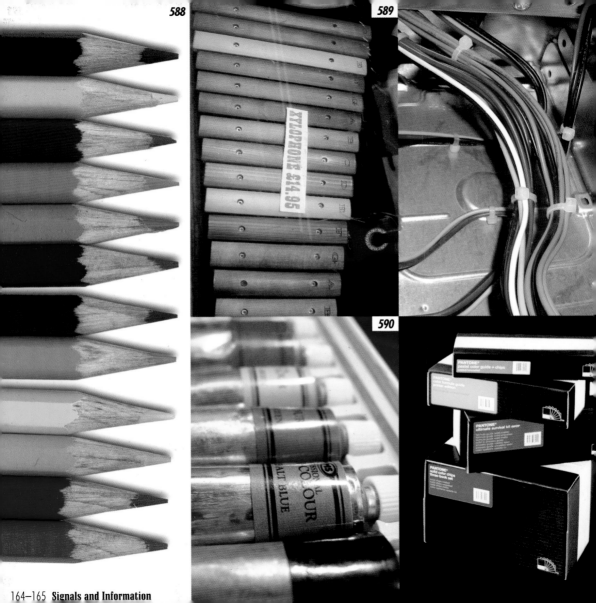

588

589

590

**588 and 590** Color choice is often indicated by stripes.
**589** "I can sing a rainbow": enjoy instant musical success with this color-coded xylophone.
**591** Follow the colored wires to ensure safe electrical repairs.
**592** Pick a color: a single bold stripe makes a powerful indicator on this simple, effective packaging for Pantone, designed by Pentagram, UK.
**593** Paula Bailey's artistic eye spotted these stripes of subtly changing hues, created by a colored cotton reel display.

**594** **595** **596**

→ Ranges that involve a vast choice are often displayed in a series of stripes. Paint color cards and reels of cotton are arranged in color groupings, creating subtle stripes of varying shades. Open a tray of colored pencils and you encounter an inspiring array of multicolored stripes. Differentiating stripes can have unusual applications: a striped xylophone makes it easier to remember the notes—just play by color.

As we scan the shelves of the supermarket, our eyes are trained to seek out goods by color. It's easier to say "get me the red one" than "get me the medium dry one." We shop by a series of visual codes, many of which are striped. Lewis Moberly's design for the Herdade do Peso wine range includes beautiful images of the flat lands of Alentejo, Portugal each one different, according to the season. These abstract landscapes create differentiating stripes, ingeniously located on the bottleneck.

**594–597** Herdade Do Peso wine packaging design by Lewis Moberly, UK. The bottle necks feature seaso striped landscapes.
**598** HEMA oils range designed by Koeweiden Postr the Netherlands.
**599–601** This range of soups from Irish food company, Erin, uses a two-tier stripe system, created Identica, UK. The landscape image is a constant, rela to the core brand's Irish countryside values. The colc coded band helps customers identify the product ran
**602** A row of flavored oils, when backlit, creates a beautiful array of colors.
**603** Yattendon Estate bread range, designed by Atelier Works, UK.

**599** **600**

"The HEMA oils project is part of an entire range of more than 250 items. The stripes are one of the patterns used as a 'palatable coding.' They have a visual reference to the food type (smearing oil on bread) and most importantly act as a signaling device. Stripes and patterns are strong visual recognition symbols. We used them in this case to categorize the different food groupings with different patterns."

*Alvin Chan,*
*Koeweiden Postma,*
*The Netherlands*

**604–606** *The famous Paul Smith stripe is used in a free-form, swirling moiré to differentiate the Paul Smith Women's range. The two stripes complement each other on men's and women's versions of his "Extreme" fragrance—designed by Paul Smith and Aboud Sodano, UK.*

605

606

**R E N CLEAN SKINCARE**

### ZOSTERA MARINA
### CLEANSING MILK WASH - DRY

**Natural Actives**
Omega 3 source **Gold of Pleasure Oil**
Pectins source **Zostera Marina**
Phytosterols source **Rose Hip Seed Oil**
Hyaluronic Acid source **Corn**

150ml ℮ / 5.1 fl.oz

**R E N CLEAN SKINCARE**

### BLACK CARDAMOM
### AND HONEY
### HAND CREAM

**Natural Actives**
Menthone source **Nepalese** Black Cardamom
Propolis source **Honey**
Glycerides source **Jojoba Oil**

**R E N CLEAN SKINCARE**

### ROSA CENTIFOLIA
### FACIAL WASH - NOR

**Natural Actives**
Polyphenols source **Centifolia Rose P**
Polysaccharides source **Aloe Vera**
Rose Otto Oil source **Damask Rose Pet**

150ml ℮ / 5.1 fl.oz

REN Clean Skincare
packaging designed by EBP, UK,
has a minimal feel—predominantly
white, with a single colored stripe
to evoke key ingredients.

CLEAN SKINCARE

10 ENZYMATIC
KIN SMOOTHING
ACIAL MASK

atural Actives

itamin C source **Barbados** Cherry

apain source **Mexican** Papaya

**R E N** CLEAN SKINCARE

## COLD PRESSED MEXICAN
## LIME AND JASMINE
## HAND WASH

**Natural Actives**

**Lime Oil** source **Cold Pressed** Mexican Limes

**Jasmine Absolute** source **Egyptian** Jasmine Blossom

**Oat Aminoacids** source **Oats**

**R E N** CLEAN SKINCARE

## MAYBLOSSOM AND BLUE
## CYPRESS FACIAL WASH -
## COMBINATION

**Natural Actives**
**Flavonoids** source **Mayblossom**
**Salicilin** source **Willow Bark**
**Guaiazulene** source **Blue Cypress Oil**

150ml e / 5.1 fl.oz

3 DESIGNER WOMENSWEAR
Designer Collections
Lingerie
Eveningwear
Disabled Toilet / Baby Changing
2 CONTEMPORARY WOMENSWEAR
Jeanswear Collections
Contemporary Fashion Brands
Contemporary Designer
Customer Services
1 ACCESSORIES
Designer Brands
-Dolce & Gabbana
-Gucci
-Yves Saint Laurent Rive Gauche
Jewellery & Watches
Women's Shoes
Fashion Accessories
Designer Gifts
Toilets
0 BEAUTY
Cosmetics
Skincare
Fragrance
Hosiery
Beauty Room
-1 MENSWEAR
Designer Brands
Casual Collections
Formal Collections
Personal Tailoring
Men's Shoes
Accessories

**608**

**609**

FITTING ROOMS

**610**

2

**611**

2 riverside

| 2 courtyard | | |
|---|---|---|
| | interior products | 2.01 |
| | accessories | 2.02 |
| | jewellery | 2.03 |
| parul & varuk | furniture & lighting | 2.04 |
| fohn design | interior space design | 2.05 |
| designblue | textiles | 2.06 |
| anna lovell quinn | design products | 2.07 |
| black + blum | furniture & design products | 2.08 |
| fusion design | jewellery | 2.09 |
| | rugs | 2.10 |
| micanda watkins & kate maestri | accessories & architectural glass | 2.11 |

| 1 courtyard | | |
|---|---|---|
| candy anthony + alex di silvestro | evening wear & illustration | 1.12 |
| alexander taylor | furniture & design products | 1.13 |
| dormitory | bed linen & nightwear | 1.14 |
| moyeni | fashion | 1.15 |
| salt | textiles | 1.16 |
| john freeman | photography | 1.17 |
| 3 fish in a tree | graphic design | 1.18 |
| odile & amanda | fashion | 1.19 |
| loud genius | knitwear | 1.20 |
| joseph joseph | glass home accessories | 1.21 |
| | girl's clothing | 1.22 |

**612**

ROCK & ROLL IS HERE TO STAY

C4

TIJUANA TAXI

HERB ALBERT & TIJUANA BRASS

D4

WHIPPED CREAM

SATISFACTION

THE ROLLING STONES

E4

**608–610** Scott Albon at Kinnersley Kent Design, UK, created this simple, strong signage system for House of Fraser, with block stripes of color denoting each floor.
**611** More block colored stripes used on the elevator guide at London's OXO Tower.
**612** Thom Watson photographed this juke box in a diner. Note how the colored stripes differentiate the artist from the song.

"The colored stripes used within the signage solution for the House of Fraser, City of London store assists in clearly navigating customers around the space and highlights the available brands on display.

Each of the five floors is represented by an appropriate color that expresses the nature and stock of that floor. The backlit directories use a single stripe to highlight the floor level, while thick, clear acrylic blocks have a strip applied to the edge which refracts, allowing the color to be viewed from various angles."

*Scott Albon,*
*Kinnersley Kent Design, UK.*

## Typography

Straight, orderly lines of type create regular stripes on the page. This occurs naturally whenever we make lists such as till receipts. Using an even type style and generous leading can increase the stripeyness of typography, creating an abstract piece of design from raw information. This kills two design birds with one stone when incorporating a great deal of statutory information into the design of a piece of packaging or communication, abstracting the copy into something simple, graphic, and striped. R Design's typographic solution for Selfridges' food range does exactly that—the information becomes the main feature of the design, all uniformly set in a consistent style against slick black.

Back to basics. When writing freehand we use lined paper to keep our thoughts on the straight and narrow. The lines on writing paper are the ultimate functional stripe, ensuring notes and ideas go from pen to paper in a neat, ordered manner —and in straight lines.

*613 Creating pattern out of information: the Malin+Goetz cosmetic packaging by 2X4, US, has a subtle stripe formed by different weights of typography.*
*614 This promotional material by Lippa Pearce, UK, for shoe company, Audley, uses typography to make two different stripes.*
*615 Peter Saville's solution for "Always Now" by Section 25 was inspired by a Berthold type catalog.*
*616 Traditional Mongolian script is written down the page —a swift style of writing that creates vertical stripes.*
*617 Type forms architectural blocks in this promotional piece for Yohji Yamamoto, art directed by Peter Saville, designed by Pentagram, UK.*
*618 Paula Bailey spotted this house making a bold statement.*

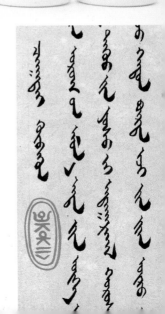

gge.{sole}
= 2.9mm/acc.
w {heel supp.} @
w.p: 52.6mm (incl.
leather) w (sole) @
w.p: 83.75mm • e.s 97
l = 258.5mm i.d = 72 ~
support = 72ø – c.j/b.s
upper shoe/2{xy}. stitch.
t {sole} = 4.4mm. ~ heel
incline = 20° raised heel
56mm {a.g.l} • a {sole}
= 11400mm² / a {heel}
= 170mm² is a{heel} =
{170/(170 + 11400)}%
of 100%. (t.s.a) wheel
centre = 50.65mm @
from shoe back ~ also
105mm from ball of
foot. wt.{shoe} = 173
gms. shoes tapers ~
max {w} ball * foot to
front. sole = i.m. nyl.
{x} ▼ inj. heel « via
‹2 spigots›. total
pmtr. of sole (l)
= 506 mm.

*relaxing*
*awhile, briefly*
*conversing - fleet*
*afoot, base balancing*
*head - striding along,*
*beating quick rhythms.*
*dextrously controlling,*
*powerfully projecting.*
*softly ensconced, phalanges*
*smooching - dawdling slowly,*
*free form, lazy, syncopation*
*naked, brazen displays,*
*signalling intent - arching*
*gracefully, supporting*
*ambition - hiding desire,*
*caressing ever discreetly*
*sheathed synthetically,*
*skin u ion skin upon skin*
*stubbing nocturnally,*
*fibulaic pogoing - tapping*
*subconsciously, mind*
*tempted by the beat*
*entwined in passion,*
*on parade in repose*
*witness to momentum,*
*carriers of all of*
*our lives*

Section 25-Always now friend
ly fires dirty disco c.p. loose tal
k costs lives inside out melt clos
e hit babies in the bardo be bra
ve new horizon produced by
martin hannett engineer joh
n caffrey recorded at brittania
row disegnatori : grafica indu
stria e typografica berthold a
factory records product fact 45

CHARDONNAY VIN DE PAYS D'OC 2001

MERLOT VIN DE PAYS D'OC 2001

PURE GROUND KENYAN GETHUMB- WINI COFFEE

sharp, bright, invigorating
strength 5

MEDIUM CUT ORANGE MARMALADE

RUNNY HONEY WITH HONEYCOMB

CRANBERY & ORANGE SAUCE

```
                              £1.19
* HARPIC LIME/S               £0.69
* PERSL BAK SODA              £1.29
* THICK BLEACH                £1.59
*20 ALL/P CLOTHS              £2.99
* JS KITCHN FOIL              £1.89
* PARCHMENT PAPR              £0.94
LINGUINE                      £1.49
ENG MARMALADE                 £0.96
ANCHOR BUTTER                 £1.42
CLIPPER F/TRADE               £0.45
PLUM TOM JUICE                £0.60
ITALIAN PASTA                 £0.35
* L/CAL TONIC                 £2.39
* JS APPLE JUICE              £0.75
JS CRACKERS                   £0.61
CORNISH WAFER                 £0.93
DEANS WDLND EGGS
PRK/APP SAUSAGE
        2 @    £2.09          £4.18
*** MULTIBUY ***            -£0.43
Cashier Confirmed - Age Over 18
* CHASSE / PAPE               £3.99
* CHASSE / PAPE               £3.99
*MOUTON CADET RD              £4.99
*MOUTON CADET RD              £4.99
* MUSCADET BOT                £2.99
*PRESTIGE DU ROC              £3.49
BUY 6 SAVE...               -£1.23
* JS HJCE BCURRT
        2 @    £1.79          £3.58
* CRANBERRY DRNK              £1.59
CAFE DIRECT                   £3.95
NCG CR TOM SOUP               £1.95
NCG CR TOM SOUP               £1.95
1 FREE                      -£1.95
ORGANIC CHEDDAR               £2.44
CORIANDER                     £0.64
MARROWFAT PEAS                £0.72
JS PESTO SAUCE                £1.46
JS PESTO SAUCE                £1.46
```

"We were briefed to design a range of products to reflect Selfridges' brand values rather than be product specific. Color coding everything black was not only corporate and stylish but also made an incredible statement on the shelf. Using only color to indicate product flavor, all the typography was set in the same face and, wherever possible, the same point size across the range. This ensured clarity, uniformity, and stunning good looks."

*David Richmond,
R Design, UK*

**619 and 620** The award-winning Selfridges' food range packaging by R Design, UK.
**621** A till receipt displays information in neat, orderly stripes.

| | |
|---|---|
| 2 @ | £1.10 |
| DAFFODILS | £0.00 |
| DAFFODILS | £1.49 |
| DWARF BEANS | £1.49 |
| BROCCOLI | £0.99 |
| 0.225 kg @ £1.89/ kg | £0.43 |
| S/C STEAK PIE | |
| 2 @ £2.79 | £5.58 |
| 1 FREE | -£2.79 |
| SPN/RIC PIZZERIA | £2.99 |
| FORMAGGI PIZZA | £2.99 |
| PEPPERONI PIZZER | |
| 2 @ £2.39 | £4.78 |
| CELERY | £0.48 |
| POINTED CABBAGE | £0.95 |
| BANANAS | |
| 0.920 kg @ £0.74/ kg | £0.68 |
| TOMATOES X6 | £0.99 |
| CARROTS | |
| 1.460 kg @ £0.54/ kg | £0.79 |
| ONIONS LARGE | |
| 0.390 kg @ £0.64/ kg | £0.25 |
| PEPPER RED | £0.74 |
| APPLE GRNNY SMTH | |
| 1.210 kg @ £1.07/ kg | £1.29 |

"Some people find it strange, but I find stripes and lines of common papers very hard to resist! And when you happen to have a fetish for old papers, stripes and lines are not at all difficult to come across... they are now so commonplace that they are almost becoming invisible.

My products are a direct result of my fascination with the stripes and lines of everyday printed language. Over several years I had accumulated many boxes of these papers which I found much too attractive not to collect. This began to get out-of-hand so I finally decided to randomly cut and bind my many papers to create limited-edition notebooks and other such items for creative types. It is my sincere hope that they will be found to be charming and inspiring.

Lines and stripes are the pathways of visual communication."

*Sharilyn Wright,*
*Lovelydesign, Canada*

**622–634** *A selection of lined and striped paper, collected and utilized in the products of Lovelydesign, Canada.*

622

623

627

631

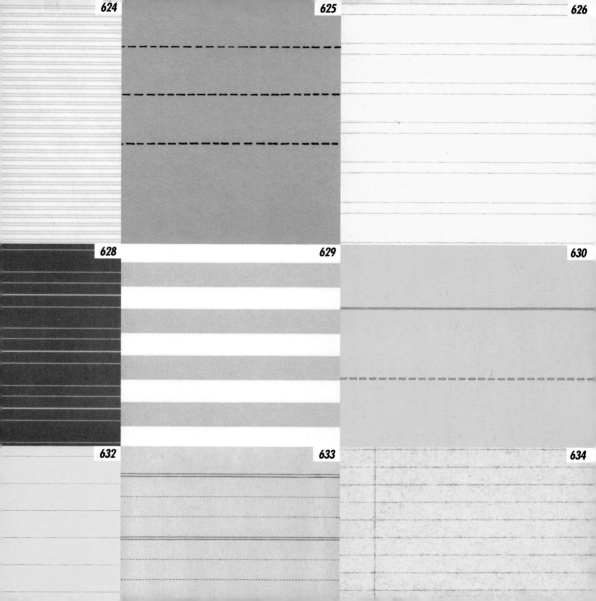

# Measurement

We measure in stripes. Whatever the unit, we count stripes on thermometers, measuring jugs, and rulers to tell us how many degrees, how many pints—even how long is a piece of string.

These are stripes of precision—fine parallel lines, equally spaced. Increments are indicated by stripes of varying lengths: a longer stripe occurs every, say, ten degrees. Awkward inches are broken down into manageable sixteenths, eighths, quarters, and halves—each increment having its own length of stripe. The American football field is known as the Gridiron

because of the lines that cross the field every five yards. Want level shelves? Use a spirit level and ensure the bubble sits equidistant between the stripes.

**635** The American football field has calibrations along its length—earning it the nickname, "Gridiron."
**636–642** Increments are measured in fine, precise stripes: a selection of measuring devices, from rulers to thermometers.

635

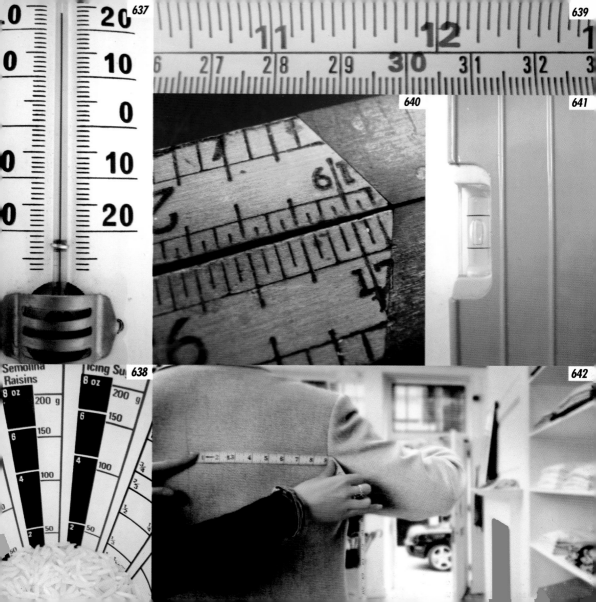

## Contours

Contours are used on maps to show the height of the land above sea. They mark out the form of hills, mountains, and valleys. When the contour lines are close together it means that the slope is steep, far apart and the slope is gentle, the number alongside the contour line indicating the height above sea level.

Maps hold a particular appeal for graphic designers—the layers of information offer a rich design language that can be creatively appropriated for non-geographic applications. Contours can be quite beautiful, especially when rendered in three dimensions, as in the Cityscape Paris rug by Hive, which recreates the soft undulations of the French capital in layers of luxurious wool felt.

Other information graphics that use series of curves include isotherms and isobars on weather maps. These are lines drawn between individual places on a map that share the same temperature or pressure ("iso" means "equal," "therm" means "temperature," and "bar" means pressure)—so they help indicate a weather pattern occurring across the country or region. Viewed with a graphic eye, these swirling lines create a striking design.          →

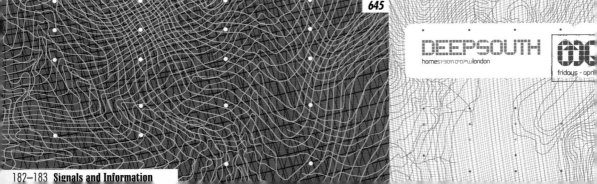

**643, 645, and 646** Promotional material
for former super club, Home, by Zip Design,
UK, using geographic reference—in
particular, contours.
**644** The Far Away writing set by
Lovelydesign, Canada, derives its charm
from its use of surplus printed maps.

**647** Cityscape Paris contoured rug by Hive,
UK. Other cities are available—best avoid
San Francisco!

→ Any instrument that records pulses and vibrations (the way a seismometer records earthquake movements) creates a series of lines and curves that can be viewed as delicate striations. Perhaps the most well-recognized pulses in popular culture are the ones that record the final flashes of the CP 1919 Pulsar (a pulsar is a cosmic source of pulsating radio signals) and adorn the cover of Joy Division's *Unknown Pleasures* album. Often called the "Dying Star" logo, the design was discovered by band member, Bernard Sumner, in a book of astrology and immortalized in Peter Saville's classic piece of sleeve design.

**648** *Elegant contours create visual interest on the feature wall of the Blue Fin Restaurant by architects, Yabu Pushelberg, Canada.*
**649** *Iconic contours from the Manchester New Wave: the sleeve of Joy Division's "Unknown Pleasures" by Peter Saville and Joy Division, UK.*

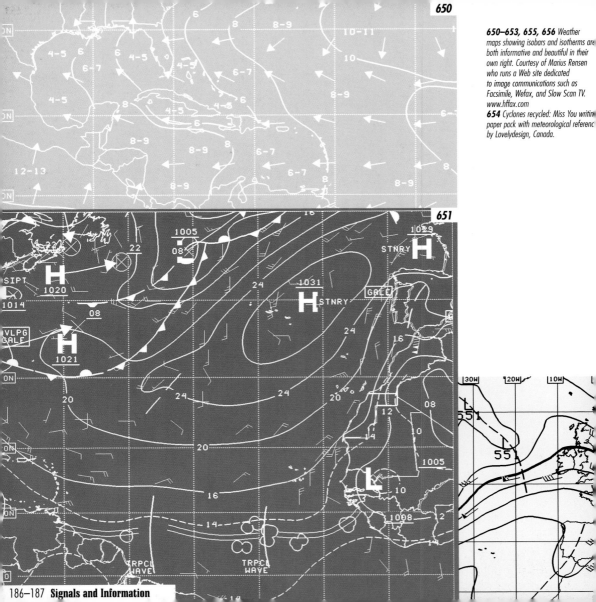

**650**

**651**

**650–653, 655, 656** Weather maps showing isobars and isotherms are both informative and beautiful in their own right. Courtesy of Marius Rensen who runs a Web site dedicated to image communications such as Facsimile, Wefax, and Slow Scan TV. www.hffax.com
**654** Cyclones recycled: Miss You writing paper pack with meteorological reference by Lovelydesign, Canada.

# Form and Function

Architecture
Cladding
Steps
Slats
Vents and Grills
Corrugation, Ribs, and Ridges
Blinds and Screens
Zippers and Seams
Wood Grain
Strata
Stacks

## Form and Function

The regular vertical slats of a white picket fence, a row of classical columns, the pressed stainless steel ridges of a draining board. All 3-D objects which, when abstracted into 2-D, create stripes. This section considers how stripes are present in the environment or in man-made products because they are intrinsic to their form or function. They give objects strength, flexibility, articulation, and protection; they turn a bland object into something sculptural, textured, and elegant. It is also about the stripes that occur naturally in wood grain or rock formations and the random stripes that can be abstracted from an arbitrary collection of objects—like a row of books or a stack of china.

Often the creation of such striped pattern is unintentional; frequently it is the by-product of structural design. Corrugated steel draws its strength and rigidity from its undulating grooves and ridges—but the play of light on the surface of the steel creates a subtly striped effect. The elbow section of a biker's jacket is ribbed to offer the protective leather improved flexibility, articulating the joint. Again, this ribbing can be seen as a structural stripe.

Here we discuss grooves, ridges, slats, beams, vents, grills, ribs, corrugation, stacks, and seams. None of them are immediately associated with stripes; all of them create a striated effect. Essentially, this is the antithesis of applied pattern—it is seeing pattern in what is already there.

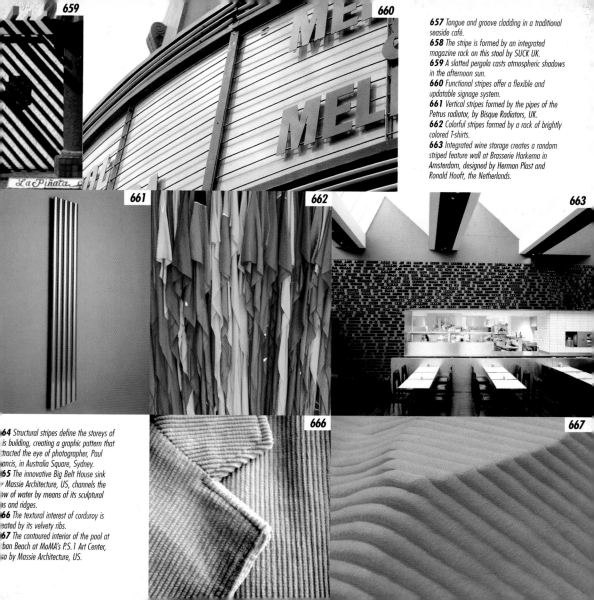

**657** Tongue and groove cladding in a traditional seaside café.

**658** The stripe is formed by an integrated magazine rack on this stool by SUCK UK.

**659** A slatted pergola casts atmospheric shadows in the afternoon sun.

**660** Functional stripes offer a flexible and updatable signage system.

**661** Vertical stripes formed by the pipes of the Petrus radiator, by Bisque Radiators, UK.

**662** Colorful stripes formed by a rack of brightly colored T-shirts.

**663** Integrated wine storage creates a random striped feature wall at Brasserie Harkema in Amsterdam, designed by Herman Plast and Ronald Hooft, the Netherlands.

**64** Structural stripes define the storeys of is building, creating a graphic pattern that tracted the eye of photographer, Paul ancis, in Australia Square, Sydney.

**65** The innovative Big Belt House sink Massie Architecture, US, channels the ow of water by means of its sculptural os and ridges.

**66** The textural interest of corduroy is eated by its velvety ribs.

**67** The contoured interior of the pool at ban Beach at MoMA's P.S.1 Art Center, o by Massie Architecture, US.

**668** The architecture of the post-war urban environment is celebrated in "Vertical Verde," a photographic transfer print on canvas by textile artist, Sharon Elphick, UK.

**669** This building gives the impression of being constructed from delicate vertical ribs.

**670** The contours of this striking building in Ecuador have been highlighted in render of contrasting sugary sweet colors.

**671 and 672** Two more buildings that successfully combine structural and esthetic considerations to create stunning striped effects in glass, concrete, and steel.

**673** A vivid green post cuts through the urban landscape to create a lone vertical stripe.

## Architecture

The urban environment is full of stripes. The construction techniques and materials used in most post-war architecture, along with a design esthetic that dictates minimal ornamentation, creates a particular geometry in glass, steel, and concrete that offers the stripe-hunter great reward. Here the very fabric of the building creates the pattern: vertical columns of concrete, load bearing girders of steel, regular horizontal expanses of glass.

Textile artist, Sharon Elphick, exploits this in her designs. Her wallpaper plays with the vertical lines of tower blocks, accentuated by overprinted stripes of lilac, lemon, green, and turquoise—a color palette of soft pastels that reflects the era when this style of architecture was at the height of its popularity.

But it it's not only modern architecture that can be abstracted by the creative eye to form stripes. Half-timbered buildings of the Middle Ages proudly display their construction technique in the form of rows of prominent supporting and bracing beams of oak, often stark black against white render, creating dizzyingly stripy results. More subtly, architecture of the classical order uses carvings and moldings that create stripes through the play of light and shade—think of the elegant flutes of classical columns, the ordered grooves in a row of capitals, or simply the repeat verticals of a colonnade—the formality of classical architecture is largely created through a dominance of stripes. →

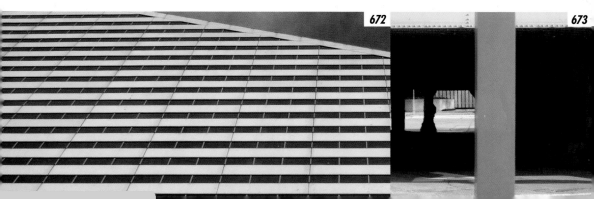

**674**

**676**

**674–680** Once you start, you can't stop: try stripe spotting around town—soon you'll be seeing stripes in architecture of every kind.
**681** This wallpaper by Sharon Elphick, UK, appears to be a purely abstract design, but in fact derives its strong geometry from graphic images of tower block apartments, overprinted in stripes of contrasting color.

**679**

682

686

687

**684**

**685**

**689**

**691**

**682–691** Subtle architectural stripes are formed by the grooves and moldings of classical architecture.

**692**

**693**

**698**

**699**

**692–703** Half-timbered houses make a feature of the construction technique. The timbers make up the frame of the building and support the weight of the roof. The spaces in between were originally filled with wattle and daub, which was left brown or painted white. The hallmark stripes of these buildings have enjoyed periods of favor since the Middle Ages, notably during the romantic Arts and Crafts movement of the early 1900s and again in the ostentatious 1980s, when the "mock tudor" mansion became synonymous with executive living.

**704**

→ Many contemporary architects looking for ways to embellish their buildings while still working within a minimalist esthetic use such "structural" stripes to create texture and visual interest without getting into superfluous decoration. The effect is of timeless elegance rather than fussy adornment—epitomized by the façade of the W Hotel in New York, designed by Canadian architects, Yabu Pushelberg.

**705**

"Stripes propel you from one place to another. The use of stripes is a fantastic way to get you (or your eyes) to move where the action continues.

Of course, Paul Smith was instrumental in bringing stripes back to the public eye. We always thought there would be an architectural way to look at the esthetic.

We incorporated it into these two projects and still continue to play with the notion on a larger scale. As people are mostly used to seeing stripes on shirts or linens, blowing it up on a much larger canvas (interiors, building facades) becomes unexpected and much more interesting."

*Stefan Boublil,*
*The Apartment, US*

**704** *Structural stripes enhance the fireplace of the Soho loft of Stefan Boublil and Gina Alvarez, founders of The Apartment, US.* **705** *W Hotel, New York, by Yabu Pushelberg, Canada: both the exterior and the signage are clad with randomly spaced 3-D stripes.* **706** *Chair rail walls make an unusual stripy texture in the lobby of Velocity, a luxury boutique condominium in New Jersey, by The Apartment, US.*

## Cladding

Architectural cladding can take on various forms—from traditional timber clapboard to modern cladding in hi-tech materials. Having evolved from the simplest timber construction techniques, cladding, which creates subtle textural stripes on the surface of a building, has an enduring appeal for architects who continue to use it for its combination of functionality and esthetic versatility.

The quaint horizontal stripes of clapboard (also referred to as weatherboard or siding) are to be found in Scandinavian architecture, often painted in rich, earthy colors; in the traditional buildings of Kent, England, in austere black or crisp white; in the colonial buildings of New England, US, in an array of tones—both vibrant and muted—exemplified by Sharon Elphick's colorful print "New England."

Clapboard was originally conceived as an effective way of providing insulation and protection to timber-constructed houses. The horizontal stripes are formed by the construction technique—the boards being laid in steps, each one overlapping the one below it, leaving a few inches exposed to the weather—thus creating a façade that will repel rainwater effectively.

These subtly rippled structures blend into the countryside, their materials and construction methods harmonious with the surrounding landscape. The award winning Black House by UK practice, Mole Architects, takes inspiration from neighboring furrowed fields, while being distinctly contemporary in its use of modern materials, applied as vertical stripes which enhance the building's elegant dimensions.

"The Black House sits in the Fen landscape, where stripes are evident in the pattern of drainage ditches to the ploughing of the black earth. This pattern-making, the consequence of containing and working the land, gives The Fens a visual quality that makes evident the history of the land's occupation. The cladding of the Black House— a cement-fiber sheet material ubiquitous on the local agricultural sheds—catches the sun in the same way as the furrows on the adjacent field."

*Meredith Bowles,*
*Mole Architects, UK*

*707, 708, and 710–712* Clapboard has been a popular construction technique for centuries. These examples span its application on styles including Kentish, New England, and 1960s modern, where it brings warmth and texture to the simple, functional architecture.
*709* The Black House by Mole Architects, UK, derives its name from the black cladding that echoes the dark furrowed fields of its Cambridgeshire Fens setting.

**713** Clapboard houses of many colors are the subject of "New England," an architectural study by textile artist Sharon Elphick, UK.
**714** Photographer Ashley Cameron captures the still beauty of these traditional Scandinavian houses.
**715** Cladding of a rather more prosaic nature.
**716** Painted clapboard complements other architectural materials and blends in with its surroundings.

713

714

715

FOR
WORKERS
ONLY

716

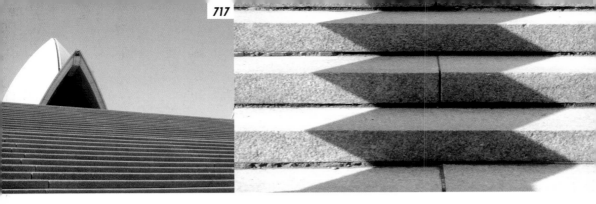

## Steps

Steps are architectural stripes, breaking physical space into a multitude of tiers and levels. In design and communication terms, steps can take on meaning beyond that of simply getting from one level to another.

Steps can evoke intrigue: where do these steps lead me as a viewer? They can suggest a journey: propelling the viewer from one space to another. They can create drama and grandeur: the image of the Sydney Opera House appearing above a bank of steps offers a wonderful sense of arrival.

The graphic representation of steps can be at once static yet dynamic, communicating both mystery and a sense of anticipation. This is used to great effect by Peter Saville, in the cover design for Architecture and Morality by OMD, which portrays a featureless urban space brought to life by the bold striped shadows cast by a fire escape.

The step also offers a useful messaging opportunity—the facing plane allows messages of information, direction, warning, or advertising—so whatever country of the world you are in, you will always emerge from a subway knowing the location of the closest McDonalds.

**717** *Sense of arrival: The Sydney Opera House peers above the steps.*
**718** *Steps with chevron shadows.*
**719** *"Architecture and Morality" by OMD, designed by Peter Saville and Brett Wicke, UK, with architecture photography by Robin Roddey.*
**720** *Inlaid marble steps create an intrigu. optical effect.*
**721** *Stair facings make stripy information panels.*
**722** *Painted wooden stairs.*
**723** *The shallower the steps, the grande the stairs.*
**724** *Railings cast striped shadows, reminiscent of the OMD sleeve.*
**725** *Metal grooves of escalators on the London Underground.*
**726** *Wooden escalators of the Moscow M*

# & MORALITY

## by
## Orchestral
## Manœuvres
## In The Dark

**ARCHITECTURE**

**727**

## Slats

From everyday fences to contemporary furniture design, slatting is a versatile construction technique that is used whenever a solid material is not required or would be too heavy. Slats let light through, allow for drainage, and create semi-, rather than total, obscurity. Slatting offers two stripes for the price of one. Firstly, there's the stripe created by the material the slat is made from, usually wood or metal, then there's the stripe created by the gap. This play of positive and negative space is what makes slatted objects so appealing.

When we think of slats, it's easy to conjure up the purely prosaic. The simplest fence can be made from rough-hewn slats of wood, evenly spaced and connected by wire. Elaborate on this design a little and you get the ubiquitous white picket fence that has become a universal symbol of contented domesticity—signifying a home (and attitude) that is neat, ordered, and conservative. Yet slats have applications way beyond the functionality of fences. Many architects and designers work with slats to create something far more graceful—and much more exclusive.

The negative space—the gap—is what really earns slatted forms their stripes, and this is often to do with the play of light and shadow.  →

**731**

**732**

"Stripes help define proportion, scale, and balance in any single design."

**Michael Heltzer,
Heltzer Furniture, US.**

**727, 731, and 734** The Scandia range, available as lounge and dining chairs, designed by Hans Brattrud in 1957, enjoys a new lease of life—reissued by fjordfiesta.furniture, Norway and distributed in the UK by Places and Spaces.

**728, 730, and 732** Slatted fences offer a simple boundary solution and a degree of charm.

**729, 735, and 736** The "Woven Trellis System" by Heltzer Furniture, US, uses its functional stripes to act as architecture, furniture, and accessory.

**733** Tidy house, tidy mind: white picket fences serve as a metaphor for conservative values.

**737, 739, and 743–745** Organic shapes and contemporary materials create a magical play of light and shade in the slatted walkways of the Urban Beach at MoMA's P.S.1 Art Center, designed by Massie Architecture, US. The original renders for the design are stripy artwork in their own right.
**738** "Dub the Mighty Dragon" by Meteorites, CD cover by Red Design, UK.
**740** The steel slats of a contemporary bridge.
**741 and 742** Similar structures, different materials: both of these canopies use slats to offer a shaded walkway, both create a delightfully striped shadow effect, but one is formed from rustic timber, the other from blades of steel.

**737**

**741**

**742**

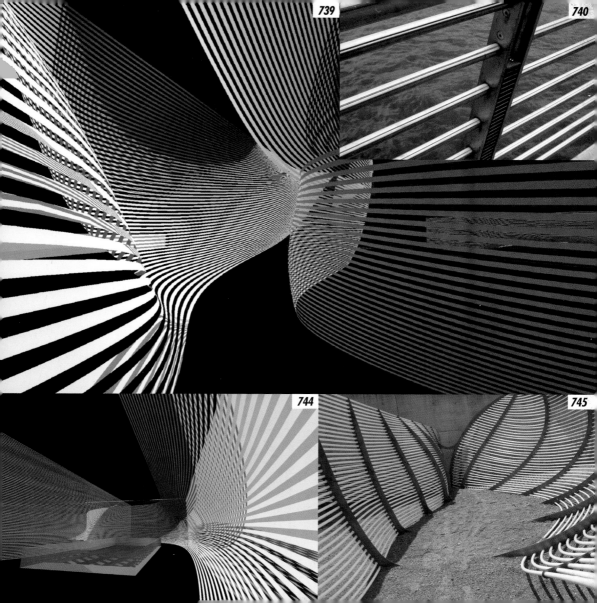

**746**

**747**

→ When light passes through slats, the result is a doubling up of the stripes—a pattern of 3-D stripes in one plane is repeated in the shadow it casts on a horizontal or opposite plane, creating interplay between the physical structure and its image. This is used to great effect by New York practice, Massie Architecture, in their design for the Urban Beach at MoMA's P.S.1 Art Center. Here, slats of PVC pipe and contoured steel create shaded spaces "blending the terms and associated ideas of surf, surface, and sensuality as they relate to the natural landscape, the urban landscape, and the landscape of the body."

Furniture made of slats has the advantage of a lightness of touch, while not compromising on strength and resilience. Take the Scandia chair— originally designed in 1957 by Norwegian, Hans Brattrud. Now faithfully

recreated and reissued, the Scandia is enjoying a revival both as a lounge chair and a dining chair. The slats offer support and strength and allow the chair a degree of stretch and movement that adds to the comfort factor, while the sleekness of its design is down to its simplicity—the elegant bent wood slats merge and diverge like contours on a map, creating a shapely form that has presence without weightiness.

The Georgie table by Brooklyn-based designers, 54Dean, is crafted out of steel and eco-friendly bamboo. Its contemporary simplicity is derived from both its sleek silhouette and the feeling of lightness created by the space between the slats. But the table holds another secret. When lit from above, the slats give rise to a mesmerizing play of graphic striped shadows.

**750**

"What excites us about the use of stripes in furniture design, in this case slat construction, is that it engages the play of light and shadow by revealing and utilizing negative space. Stripes projected upon a room enhance the visual interaction between furniture and its environment."

*Todd Seidman,*
*54Dean, US*

**752**

**746 and 751** *Metal slats used on everyday street furniture and park benches.*
**747 and 748** *The Breakform bench by 54Dean, US, demonstrates how slats offer elegance and practicality for outdoor furniture. They lighten the design, offering improved portability, and they allow water to drain through during winter months of outdoor storage.*
**749, 750, and 752** *Shadow play: the Georgie bench casts myriad stripes on its surroundings. The piece derives its name from design godfather, George Nelson, a major influence on Brooklyn-based design group, 54Dean, US.*

## Vents and Grills

Vents and grills form protective stripes—both physical and metaphorical. Take physical protection first. Erected in front of vulnerable objects, fragile surfaces, and dangerous places, grills are a form of guard. A set of parallel metal bars will protect a window against unwanted intrusion or can prevent you from falling down a drain. Vents allow the flow of air or sound through molded grooves of plastic or metal, while protecting the mechanism within the appliance. Designers can exploit this functional necessity and make a virtue out of vented design—either in product design, where vents can communicate raw functionality or in graphic design that draws inspiration from the industrial chic of vent and grill structures.

Many vents are designed to allow one-way air-flow, either for purposes of expelling moisture or odors from the atmosphere, or for the intake of cooling air to protect mechanisms. These vents are often more sophisticatedly molded to create a hooded element—giving rise to a different form of stripe. →

*753–755* Sound vents on radios and intercoms.
*756, 758, 759, and 763* Air vents ensure efficient cooling of machinery and engines.
*757, 761, and 762* Protective grills over drains facilitate water drainage.
*760* 1980 sleeve design by Peter Saville and Ben Kelly, UK, for the album, "Orchestral Manoeuvres in the Dark," takes inspiration from the industrial chic of the grill. Its pull-out inner sleeve reveals the die-cut outer component.

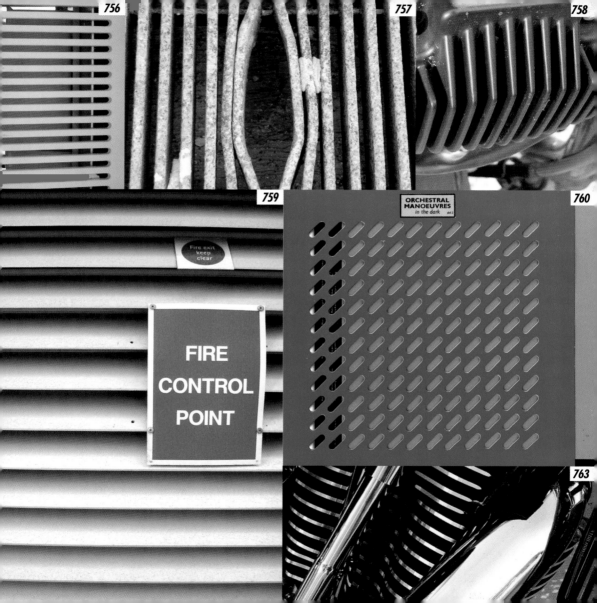

756

757

758

759

Fire exit
keep
clear

FIRE
CONTROL
POINT

ORCHESTRAL
MANOEUVRES
in the dark

760

763

764

765

769

DANGER
PROTECTED BY RAZOR WIRE

GAGGENAU

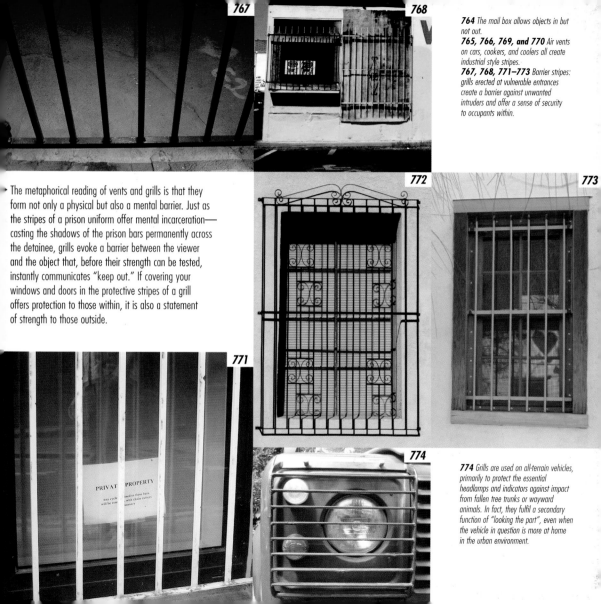

**767**

**768**

**764** The mail box allows objects in but not out.
**765, 766, 769, and 770** Air vents on cars, cookers, and coolers all create industrial style stripes.
**767, 768, 771–773** Barrier stripes: grills erected at vulnerable entrances create a barrier against unwanted intruders and offer a sense of security to occupants within.

The metaphorical reading of vents and grills is that they form not only a physical but also a mental barrier. Just as the stripes of a prison uniform offer mental incarceration—casting the shadows of the prison bars permanently across the detainee, grills evoke a barrier between the viewer and the object that, before their strength can be tested, instantly communicates "keep out." If covering your windows and doors in the protective stripes of a grill offers protection to those within, it is also a statement of strength to those outside.

**772**

**773**

**771**

PRIVATE PROPERTY

Any cycle ___ned to these bars
will be rem___ with chain cutters
___ necessary

**774**

**774** Grills are used on all-terrain vehicles, primarily to protect the essential headlamps and indicators against impact from fallen tree trunks or wayward animals. In fact, they fulfil a secondary function of "looking the part", even when the vehicle in question is more at home in the urban environment.

## Corrugation, Ribs, and Ridges

Form and function come together in corrugated surfaces. Corrugated metal is a type of sheet iron or steel, strengthened by having a series of alternating grooves and ridges forced into it—thus creating the impression of stripes. Corrugation offers strength to weak materials and flexibility to rigid materials. So corrugated cardboard can withstand the forces of transporting heavy objects and corrugated plastic can be bent and molded into complex shapes.

As Tom Dixon mentions in reference to his wonderfully simple extendable screen (which he describes as an "all-purpose snaky dividing wall"), stripes are a by-product of the corrugation or ribbing. These are "self" stripes—not created by surface printing or juxtaposition of materials—they are present as a result of the play of light on a ribbed or pleated surface and intrinsic to a product's construction.

Corrugated card in its raw form is often used to communicate honest and down-to-earth values in packaging such as that for the Dr. Martens Useful Clothing range. Its striped ribs say "no frills here, just good, basic product that works." It's a sophisticated marketing message that feels effortless. →

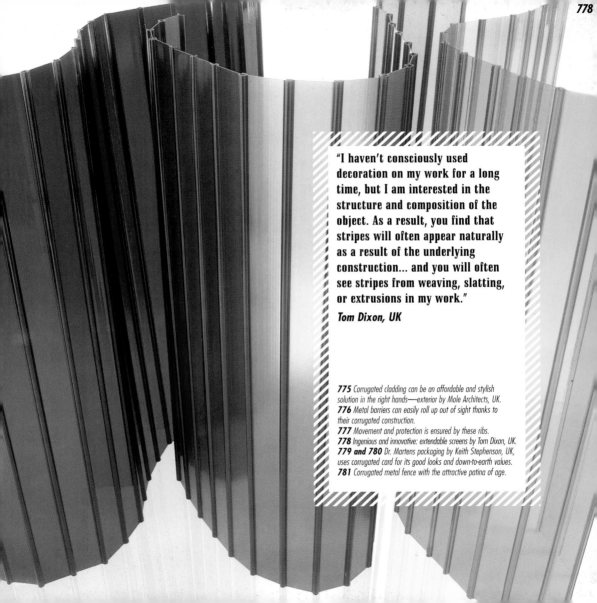

"I haven't consciously used decoration on my work for a long time, but I am interested in the structure and composition of the object. As a result, you find that stripes will often appear naturally as a result of the underlying construction... and you will often see stripes from weaving, slatting, or extrusions in my work."

*Tom Dixon, UK*

**775** Corrugated cladding can be an affordable and stylish solution in the right hands—exterior by Mole Architects, UK.
**776** Metal barriers can easily roll up out of sight thanks to their corrugated construction.
**777** Movement and protection is ensured by these ribs.
**778** Ingenious and innovative: extendable screens by Tom Dixon, UK.
**779 and 780** Dr. Martens packaging by Keith Stephenson, UK, uses corrugated card for its good looks and down-to-earth values.
**781** Corrugated metal fence with the attractive patina of age.

**782** A bendy bus with its central panel of articulation stripes.
**783** Conduit piping is ribbed for flexibility when being fed through underground tunnels.
**784** The beauty of corrugated cladding, used in an industrial setting, is caught in this photograph by Kyle E. Chambers.
**785 and 787** Bikers display their ribs: protective leathers all have stripy ribs for flexible joints.
**786** Bendy straws work on the same principle: strength and flexibility are offered by their ribbed construction.

→ Ribbing offers flexibility to materials like leather and plastic—so it is used to articulate the arm joints of protective clothing, offering movement without compromising on strength. The stripes created on these garments look technical and efficient, and add to the overall design appeal. Another example of articulation stripes is in the increasingly prevalent "bendy bus." It bends in the middle, aided by the concertina construction of this crucial central section.

Maximizing surface area is key to effective heat radiation—hence the ridged and ribbed form of radiators. In the kind of radiators to be found in old Victorian buildings, this was achieved by rows of interconnected vertical pipes creating structures so sturdy you could stand on them to open the window. More recently, ridged sheets of pressed steel have become the norm, which make for effective heat conduction, but rather less grand appliances. But what all radiators, old and new, have in common is that their ridges, ribs, and pipes create 3-D stripes. Contemporary manufacturers like Bisque have wised up to the potential of radiators as interior adornment rather than ugly necessity. Gone are the utilitarian ribs of 1970s radiators in favor of elegant, striated forms that earn the right to be wall mounted, taking center stage in a contemporary design scheme, complementing or even taking the place of wall-hung art pieces.

**791**

**793**

**788–791, 793, and 794**
An architectural radiator can be a feature of a room or be integral to its interior design. This collection from Bisque Radiators, UK, shows that they no longer have to be hidden behind fret-cut covers.
**792** Even a conventional radiator can cut a dash with an architectural stripe.

**792**

**794**

## Blinds and Screens

The simplest way of creating a doorway screen is to hang vertical strips of colored vinyl—the type that used to adorn the doorways of greengrocers in the 1960s. Gently floating in the hot summer breeze, these multicolored stripes have a retro appeal, redolent of childhood shopping trips.

Equally evocative are the stripes formed by Venetian blinds—so called because their horizontal slatted design is thought to have first appeared in Venice in the late 18th century. Not only are they a classic window dressing, but also their form—and especially the stripy shadows they cast across an interior scene—has become a widely used photographic and cinematic motif. In film noir, Venetian blinds create an air of moody tension. There's something suggestive about Venetian blinds—something about the way they offer just a glimpse of a scene. Thus, their graphic shadows have been used to evoke seedy motel room sex, or general promiscuity, typified by the film poster for the 1980 film *American Gigolo*, starring Richard Gere. →

**795** *Vinyl strip curtains are colorful, practical, and just a bit retro.*
**796** *Two realities in one image: promotional material by NB:Studio, UK, for the film "Requiem for a Dream," juxtaposes two images in fine alternating vertical strips to create a sense of narrative and insight.*
**797** *Louvred doors draw Spanish influences.*
**798** *Detail of vertical blinds.*
**799** *Advertising images applied to a phone box in fine horizontal stripes create the impression of a full image from the outside and allow a view out from the inside.*

800

803

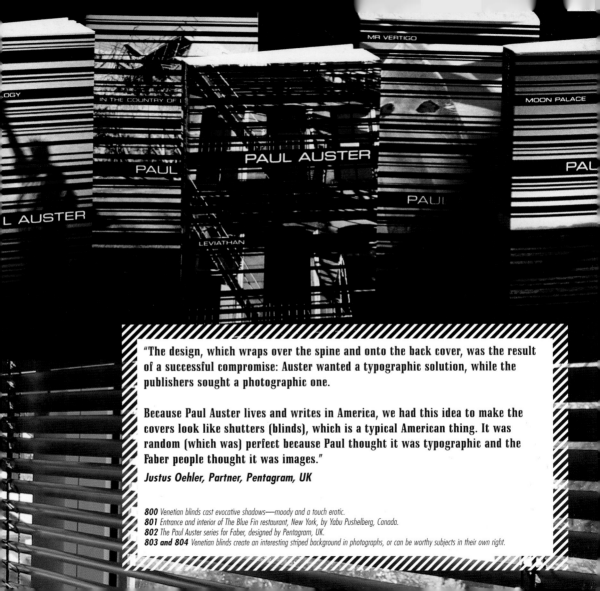

"The design, which wraps over the spine and onto the back cover, was the result of a successful compromise: Auster wanted a typographic solution, while the publishers sought a photographic one.

Because Paul Auster lives and writes in America, we had this idea to make the covers look like shutters (blinds), which is a typical American thing. It was random (which was) perfect because Paul thought it was typographic and the Faber people thought it was images."

*Justus Oehler, Partner, Pentagram, UK*

**800** Venetian blinds cast evocative shadows—moody and a touch erotic.
**801** Entrance and interior of The Blue Fin restaurant, New York, by Yabu Pushelberg, Canada.
**802** The Paul Auster series for Faber, designed by Pentagram, UK.
**803 and 804** Venetian blinds create an interesting striped background in photographs, or can be worthy subjects in their own right.

808

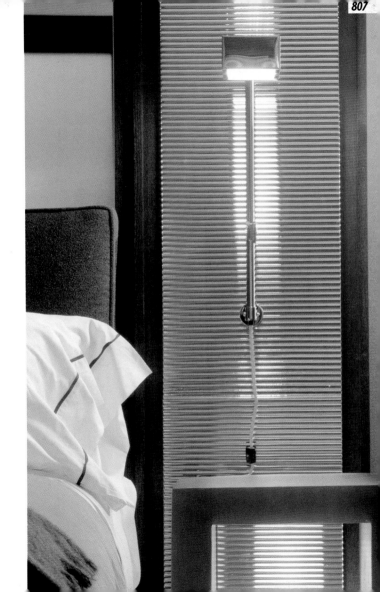

In interior design, the many individual slats of screens and blinds have the benefit of creating partial obscurity while allowing the light to filter through. They enable a large area to be divided into smaller, more intimate zones, without losing the overall sense of space—perfect in restaurants, bars, and hotel lobbies, whether the esthetic is sharp contemporary or relaxed colonial. This makes for a kind of semi-privacy, similar to that offered by ridged glass: a half-way house between the opaque and the transparent. Ridged glass refracts light so that figures viewed through it become instantly striated, adding to the visual drama of any space.

**805** *The lobby of the W Hotel, Times Square, New York by Yabu Pushelberg, Canada, uses ingenious dividing screens that combine privacy and light.*
**806 and 808** *Late afternoon sun through Venetian blinds creates a calm atmosphere.*
**807** *Ridged glass offers textural interest to this hotel room by Yabu Pushelberg, Canada.*
**809** *En-suite facilities tucked discretely behind louvred doors.*

**21 August to
5 October 2003**

Crafts Council Gallery
44a Pentonville Road
London N1 9BY

Free Entry
Tuesday to Saturday 11–6
Sunday 2–6 Closed Monday

Disabled Access &
www.craftscouncil.org.uk
3 minutes from Angel
Telephone 020 7278 7700

Alexander Beleschenko
Katharine Coleman
Matthew Durran
Amber Hiscott
Angela Jarman
Helen Maurer
Colin Rennie
Koichiro Yamamoto

810

# JERWOOD APPLIED ARTS PRIZE 2003 GLASS

**810, 815, 816** NB:Studio, UK, designed this Crafts Council promotional material for the Glass section of the Jerwood Applied Arts prize. Its use of ridged glass not only ties in with the subject matter, but also exploits its striking distorting effects—transforming an image into a series of repeated stripes.
**811** Interior of the W Hotel, Times Square, New York by Yabu Pushelberg, Canada.
**812–814** Ridged glass offers the perfect combination of light and privacy.

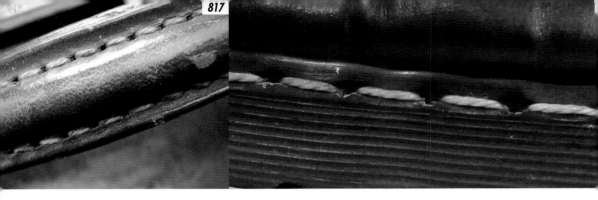

## Zippers and Seams

The zipper revolutionized clothing and fashion. Given its current popularity, it's hard to believe that when it was first introduced it was a commercial flop for the first 30 years of its life. Not until the 1920s did it achieve mainstream success, when it appeared mainly on zip-up galoshes. It was the French fashion designers of the late 1930s who finally championed the zipper as an alternative to the button fly in men's pants—and we haven't looked back since. Once it took off, it became the first truly unisex fastening. Zippers are functional but they also have sexy overtones—a sort of stripe of opportunity running right down the front of a garment offering instant, fumble-free access to the body underneath. Thus, zippers often adorn garments with a fetishist edge—think of Emma Peel's catsuit in TV series *The Avengers*.

Seams are a much more practical thing—they hold things together. But certain fashion designers and brands have gone one stage further and made a virtue of necessity—elevating the humble seam into a stripe of distinction. The instantly recognizable yellow stitching on Dr. Martens boots is one of the brand's key trademarks. Evisu creates value and desirability in its jeans by manufacturing them from denim woven on 40-year-old looms, which create a "clean" selvedge—a stripe down the edge of the fabric, often in a contrasting color, such as red. When you turn the jean up you see the two selvedge edges of the denim stitched together. This stripe is also visible on the inside of the coin pocket, adding to the covetable nature of these denim products.

**817** Leather goods require robust stitching.
**818** Distinctive yellow stitching on the Dr. Martens welted sole is part of the brand's iconography.
**819** Sought-after Evisu selvedge denim commands a premium.
**820–822** Zippers are instant-access stripes.

823

829

826

"The Strata table's simple oak legs serve as both the support and a visual frame for the boldly striped top made up from strips of different woods. The top will vary from batch to batch depending on quantity and types of wood being used in the workshop at that time with the appeal of one never looking quite the same as the last."

*Ed Carpenter, UK*

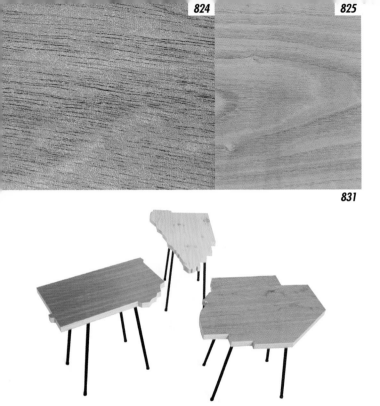

## Wood Grain

Wood grain produces natural stripes and moirés—each one unique, according to species, age, and origin. Wood veneer production methods vary—there are a number of different cutting methods, including crown cut (which tends to create a variegated grain) and quarter cutting, where the log is cut with the blade at right angles to the growth rings, creating a distinctly striped effect.

In their Strata table, Ed Carpenter and Tom Spain exploit the wealth of varied wood grains. The table is constructed out of strips of different woods to create a lively, striped design that works in both contemporary and traditional settings, and offers diners the added advantage of an enjoyable after dinner pastime: naming each of the individual types of timber.

The uniquely striped pattern of wood grain can be used to communicate age, wisdom, and experience, based on the fact that the rings of a tree indicate its age in years. Wood grain is used to bring warmth to furniture and interior schemes. It seems to have an emotional warmth that evokes simplicity and honesty.

→

828

**823** Teak veneer.
**824** Brazilian mahogany veneer.
**825** Crown cut chestnut veneer.
**826** Beech veneer.
**827** Crown cut sapele veneer.
**828** Crown cut oak veneer.
**829** The Strata table by Ed Carpenter, UK, and Tom Spain of Rushton Brothers, UK, with oak legs and top of various woods.
**830** Table mats by Ella Doran, UK, use photographs of wood veneers to create a contemporary feel.
**831** National Park tables, for the Cabin project, by Todd Falkowsky, Canada.

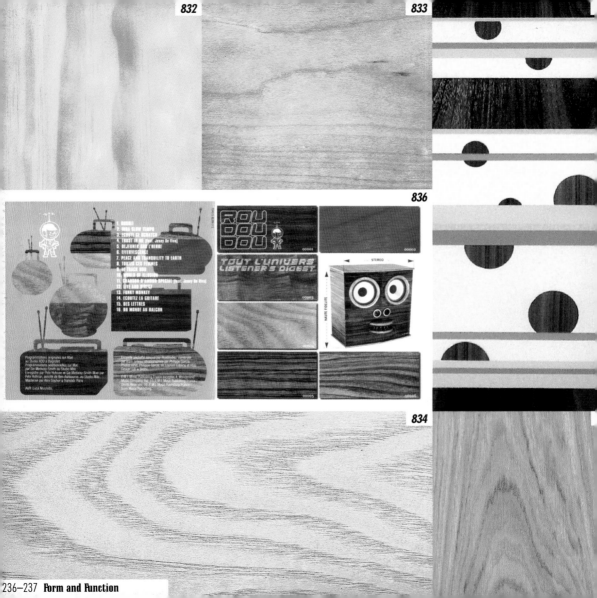

832

833

836

834

838

"The use of stripes in the Legna Wall Graphic series is a product of my desire to create a sense of order, balance, and calm. Stripes of varying widths and colors create a diorama of spatial relationships that evoke those found in a thoughtfully designed modern environment.

The result is a healthy symbiosis where all objects are of equal importance and necessity. Painting, table, lamp, and chair work as one to create a harmonious and unified environment."

*Joe Futschik,*
*jef designs, US*

**832** Pine veneer. **833** American cherry veneer.
**834** American white ash veneer.
**835** Crown cut European oak veneer.
**836** Designer, Lili Fleury, France, uses veneer sample catalogs to great effect in the charming and beautiful artwork for Tout L'Univers Listener's Digest by Roudoudou.
**837–839** The Legna Wall Graphic series by Joe Futschik from Velocity Art and Design, US.

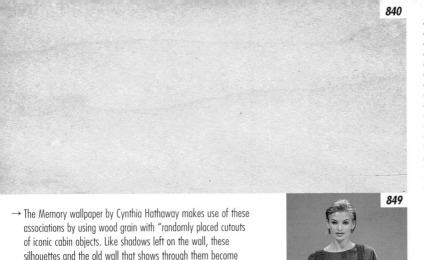

840 Maple veneer.
841 Crown-cut brown oak veneer.
842 Crown-cut plain Swiss pear veneer.
843 American cherry veneer.
844 Straight-grain European oak veneer.
845 Straight-grain American light oak veneer.
846 Lacewood veneer.
847 Straight-grain European walnut veneer.
848 Crown-cut American cherry veneer.
849 Dévoré wood grain dress, by Wayne and Gerardine Hemingway for Red or Dead, UK.
850 Tori Gardner at Camp Apparel, US, also uses wood grain on fabric in her range of fashion accessories. This Faux Wood pouch is designed, she says, "for the woodshop genius or anyone who wants to add organic flair to their look."
851 Memory Wallpaper by Cynthia Hathaway, Canada, shows tokens of cabin nostalgia, for the Cabin project.
852 Slot chair by Sebastian Bergne, Italy and UK, manufactured by Varaschin.
853 Café interior, shot by photographer, Ashley Cameron.

→ The Memory wallpaper by Cynthia Hathaway makes use of these associations by using wood grain with "randomly placed cutouts of iconic cabin objects. Like shadows left on the wall, these silhouettes and the old wall that shows through them become links to a past both real and imagined."

Many contemporary designers use wood grain or graphic representations of wood grain in their work. Hand-drawn wood grain has a naïve appeal—it can make a technical object appear home-spun; applied as a photorealistic print to laminates and fabrics, wood grain has a modern-retro edge that is graphically playful with an unexpected twist.

**849**

**843**

**844**

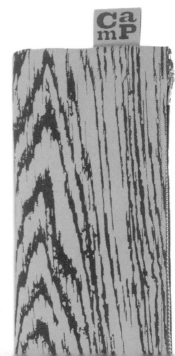

851

841

842

852

853

845

846

847

848

854

## Black Ven - Section

Modified from Davies (1935; 1956)

Ian West 2001

S.

OLD ROAD CUTTING

CHERT

FOXMOL

COWSTO

GREEN AMMONITE BED

BELEMNITE MARLS

BLACK VEN MARL

SHALES-WITH-BEEF

Belemnite Stone

Stellare Nodules

Birchi Nodules

SECTION THROUGH THE EASTERN PART OF BLACK VEN.

Farther west the Gault oversteps the Green Ammonite Beds and rests on the Belemnite

*G I S*

Burning Cliff

Geology of the The

Between Lyme Regis and Black Ven
(ENE of Lyme Regis). With Lias bed
Part of: Lang, W.D. 1913. Geological Ma
Between Charmouth and Lyme Regis.

858

859

240–241 **Form and Function**

# Strata

Stripes are to be seen on a monumental level in large rock formations such as the Grand Canyon. Here, each of the striped rock strata signifies the passage of a geological era, going back around two billion years—the result of ancient volcanic activity, marine, and river deposits, and compacted sand dunes. Mineral deposits color the various layers so that they show up from buff (Kaibab Limestone) to white (Coconino Sandstone) to purple (Temple Butte Limestone) to pink (Zoroaster Granite)—with each geological era distinctly layered like the ingredients of a club sandwich.

These stripes are a source of inspiration not only for historians and geologists who can use them to trace climactic change, but also photographers and designers. The notion of layers and strata was taken one step further in The Chase's award-winning chiseled design for Jason Orton's book, *Coastal Erosion*, bringing an innovative 3-D design solution to support the subject matter.

Coastal Erosion

**854 and 858** *Stalactites and rock formations in a cave.*
**859** *The intriguing form of the Three Sisters rock formation, Australia, displays its strata.*
**855 and 860** *Stunning shots of Arizona, US, where layers of different rock are clearly delineated.*
**856 and 857** *The ection drawn through the eastern part of the Black Ven and the Geology of The Spittles, both drawn by Dr Ian West in a study of the geology of the Wessex Coast of the UK.*
**861** *Jason Orton's "Coastal Erosion," designed by The Chase, UK.*

## Stacks

Stacks, racks, and rows of everyday objects like books, clothes, and crockery all form graphic stripes. This creates an enjoyable dilemma when it comes to arranging your book or vinyl collection. How to sort them? Alphabetically? By genre? The stripe aficionado is more likely to deliberate between organizing them into rows of block color versus the delight of forming random multicolored stripes—such as the ones that adorn accessories by designer, Ella Doran. At first glance, these appear to be printed with a set of broken stripes in contrasting colors. Closer inspection reveals that these stripes are, in fact, a photographic representation of rows of books and magazine spines.

More striped stack inspiration comes in the shape of Deborah Bowness's The Original Fake Bookshelf wallpaper, which creates a *trompe l'oeil* of shelves filled with rows of books and files. The overall effect is of a lively jostle of horizontal and vertical stripes while its restrained tonal composition ensures that the stripes neither dominate nor cause too much visual chaos.

*862 and 865* Ella Doran, UK, uses found stripes, formed by stacks of books and vinyl records on her accessory ranges of notebooks and interior products.
*863* A pile of encyclopedia, alphabetically color-coded, forms interesting stripes.
*864* Deborah Bowness, UK, exploits stack stripes in her wallpaper designs, seen here in Soho House, London, UK.
*866* A row of paperbacks forms stripes with subtle differences in color and texture.

867

871

872

875

874

**867 and 868** Two vinyl obsessives create an interesting multicolored wall of stripes.
**869 and 870** Two designs that exploit the "old school" vinyl stripe: CD cover for the American release of Fat Boy Slim's "You've come a long way, baby" by Red Design, UK, and accessories by UK designer, Ella Doran.
**871** Smart contemporary gray stripes of stacked felt are used in the construction of the Joseph Bench by 521 Design, US.
**872–877** Greetings cards, magazines, and clothes all create colorful random stripes when stacked or racked in tight formation—it's up to the viewer to abstract them.

**878, 880, and 881** Stacks of stripes: fabric, clothing, and deckchairs, all individually striped items themselves, are stacked to create 3-D stripes.

**880**

**881**

**882**

URK NOV 1989

URK DEZ. 1994

URK FEB. 1991

URK SEPT. 1991

URK SEPT.1993

URK SEPT.1993

**885**

Paris furniture fair

Paris furniture fair
rn | Bilbao | Stockholm furniture fair
rn | Bilbao | Stockho
aches | Capsule living | Swish Alps | Rio lounging
hers | Tokyo temple | Architects birectory | Tu
hidorm reborn | The Vignellis | Coffee table chi
arasota treasures | Desirable dens | African p
m | Martin Parr | Circus chic | London retail
e extensions | Hi-tech house | Venice Bien
pired and the undiscovered

**886**

*879 and 882–886 Regardless of scale, items that are all around us, from shopping carts to crockery, viewed with an imaginative eye, can form interesting bands of color.*

# Appendix

# Index

# Contributors
## Featured Designers and Suppliers

**2x4**
www.2x4.org

**54 Dean**
www.54dean.com

**521 Design**
www.fivetwentyonedesign.com

**Aboud Sodano**
www.aboud-sodano.com

**Absolute Zero°**
www.absolutezerodegrees.com

**Adidas**
www.adidas.com

**agnès b**
www.agnesb.com

**Alexander Taylor**
www.alexandertaylor.com

**All Zones**
www.allzones.com

**The Apartment**
www.theapt.com

**Art Meets Matter**
www.artmeetsmatter.com

**Atelier Works**
www.atelierworks.co.uk

**B & B Italia**
www.bebitalia.it

**Bars & Stripes**
www.barsnstripes.com

**Ben Kelly Design**
www.benkellydesign.com

**Bisque**
www.bisque.co.uk

**Brasserie Harkema**
www.brasserieharkema.nl

**Camp Apparel**
www.campapparel.com

**Cabin project**
www.motherbrand.com

**The Chase**
www.thechase.co.uk

**Comfort Station**
www.comfortstation.co.uk

**The Conran Shop**
www.conran.com

**Crystal Barlow**
www.crystalbarlow.com

**Daniel Buren**
www.danielburen.com

**Daniel Wooddell**
dano@gravityfeed.net

**Deborah Bowness**
www.deborahbowness.com

**DidjLIGHT**
www.didjlight.de

**Dr Ian West**
www.soton.ac.uk/~imw/index.htm

**Dulux**
www.dulux.co.uk

**EBP**
www.ebpcreative.com

**Ed Carpenter**
www.edcarpenter.co.uk

**Ella Doran**
www.elladoran.co.uk

**Evisu**
www.evisu.com

**Farrow and Ball**
www.farrowandball.com

**Fired Earth**
www.firedearth.com

**Fjord Fiesta**
www.fjordfiesta.com

**Fox Brothers and Co.**
www.foxflannel.com

**HF - Fax**
www.hffax.com

**Heltzer Furniture**
www.heltzer.com

**Hemingway Design**
www.hemingwaydesign.com

**Herman Prast**
www.prast.nl

**Hive**
www.hivespace.com

**homeArama**
www.homearama.co.uk

**Ian Mankin**
109 Regents Park Road
Primrose Hill, London
NW1 8UR UK
Tel +44 (0) 2077220997

**Identica**
www.identica.com

**Jean Paul Gaultier Perfumes, Kenneth Green Associates**
www.kennethgreenassociates.co.uk

**Joe Futschik**
www.velocityartanddesign.com

**Kinnersley Kent Design**
www.kkd.co.uk

**Koeweiden Postma**
www.koeweidenpostma.com

**Lance Wyman**
www.lancewyman.com

**Lewis Moberly**
www.lewismoberly.com

**Lili Fleury**
www.lilifleury.com

**Lippa Pearce**
www.lippapearce.com

**Lucienne Day**
www.twentytwentyone.com

**Luke J. Tornatzky**
www.lukejtornatzky.com

**Lovelydesign**
www.lovelydesign.com

**Marimekko**
www.marimekko.fi

**Massie Architecture**
www.massiearchitecture.com

**Meta Design**
www.metadesign.de

**Minale Tattersfield**
www.mintat.co.uk

**Mole Architects**
www.molearchitects.co.uk

**NB:Studio**
www.nbstudio.co.uk

**NYC Bloggers**
www.nyc.bloggers.com

**Natura Design Solutions**
www.naturadesignsolutions.com

**Non-Format**
www.nonformat.com

**North**
www.northdesign.co.uk

**Northern Sun**
www.northernsun.com

**Paul Smith**
www.paulsmith.com

**Penguin Books**
www.penguin.co.uk

**Pentagram**
www.pentagram.com

**Peter Saville**
www.saville-associates.com

**Places and Spaces**
www.placesandspaces.com

**R Design**
www.r-website.co.uk

**Red Design**
www.red-design.co.uk

**REN Ltd**
www.renskincare.com

**Rimmington Vian**
www.rimmingtonvian.co.uk

**Rob Hare**
www.robhare.co.uk

**Roudoudou**
www.roudoudou.fr

**Rune Mortensen Design Studio**
www.runemortensen.no

**Scott Blake**
www.barcodeart.com

**Sebastian Bergne**
www.sebastianbergne.com

**Sharon Elphick**
www.sharonelphick.com

**Social Suicide**
www.socialsuicide.co.uk

**Some**
www.some.ca

**Squires & Company**
www.squirescompany.com

**SUCK UK**
www.suck.uk.com

**Swedese**
www.swedese.se

**T.G. Green, Tabletop Group**
www.ttctabletop.com

**Thomas Pink**
www.thomaspink.co.uk

**The Original Breton Shirt Company**
www.bretonshirt.com

**The Standard, Downtown LA**
550 South Flower at Sixth Street
Los Angeles CA 90071 USA
Tel +1 213 892 8080
www.standardhotel.com

**Tom Dixon**
www.tomdixon.net

**Transport for London**
www.tfl.gov.uk

**Urban Mercantile**
www.urbanmercantile.com

**Visopia**
www.visopia.com

**Wojtek Kozak**
www.wkozak.com

**Wolff Olins**
www.wolffolins.com

**Yabu Pushelberg**
Tel +1 416 778 9779

**YSL Beauté**
Tel +44 (0) 1444255700

**Zip Design Ltd**
www.zipdesign.co.uk

# Photography Credits
## By image number

**Cover**
Inside back L/R: *Kenji Szczepanski, Keith Stephenson, Dana Damewood.* Back cover L/R: *Helen Rickard, Keith Stephenson, Toby Bradbury, Keith Stephenson.* Front cover L/R: *Keith Stephenson, Kyle E. Chambers, Teresa Lenihan, Paul Francis.* Inside front L/R: *Keith Stephenson, Paula Bailey, Keith Stephenson, Keith Stephenson, Keith Stephenson.*

**Title page**
For photography credits see repeated image numbers: L/R: **368, 272, 093, 679, 336, 795, 880, 225, 133.**

**Contents**
For photography credits see repeated image numbers: L/R: **444, 302, 635, 490, 331, 459, 669, 433, 396, 478, 080, 487.**

**Classic Stripes**
**004** *Alan Hunns*
**007** *Keith Stephenson*
**014** *Keith Stephenson*
**026** *Alison Chappell*
**027** *Ray Main*
**046–060** *Toby Bradbury*
**063** *Lyn Dafis*
**075, 076, 078–081** *Alan Hunns*

**Membership and Identity**
**091** *Paul Francis*
**093** *Roy Caratozzolo III*
**094** *Paul Francis*
**095** *Kyle E.Chambers*
**096** *Keith Stephenson*
**097** *Mark Hampshire*
**099** *Keith Stephenson*
**103** *Keith Stephenson*
**104** *Keith Stephenson*
**107** *Mark Hampshire*
**108** *Luke Williams*
**109** *Debra Horng*
**110** *Roy Caratozzolo III*
**111** *Ben Bishop*
**112** *Keith Stephenson*
**121 and 122** *Keith Stephenson*
**123** *Kenji Szczepanski*
**132** *Paul Francis*
**133** *Paul Francis*
**134** *Keith Stephenson*
**163** *Keith Stephenson*
**222** *Keith Stephenson*
**223** *Gianna Taverna*
**225** *Lucy Zhang*
**226** *Keith Stephenson*
**227** *Karol Miles*
**228** *Frank Meeuwsen*
**229** *Keith Stephenson*
**231** *Keith Stephenson*
**232** *Kyle E.Chambers*
**242** *Chris Moore*
**243** *Keith Stephenson*
**244 and 245** *Mark Jarrell*

**Themes and Moods**
**267** *Teresa Lenihan*
**268** *Keith Stephenson*
**270** *Mark Hampshire*
**272** *Mark Hampshire*
**274** *Baranaby Welch*
**275** *Paul Francis*
**279** *Dulux*
**282 and 283** *Keith Stephenson*
**284** *Ronny Bagdadi*
**285** *Lissa Hahn*
**292** *Dulux*
**293** *Mark Hampshire*
**296** *D'Arcy Norman*
**300** *Robert Sharl*
**301** *Helen Rickard*
**302 and 303** *Keith Stephenson*
**306 and 307** *Keith Stephenson*
**312** *Paul Sims*
**314 and 315** *Keith Stephenson*
**316** *Helen Rickard*
**317** *Keith Stephenson*
**318** *James Petersen*
**319** *Paul Francis*
**321** *Shannon Loewen*
**322** *Karol Miles*
**323** *Servee Schellinx*
**324–327** *Keith Stephenson*
**328** *Adam Horan*
**329** *Keith Stephenson*
**330** *James Ross*
**331** *Ian Rippington*
**333** *Teresa Lenihan*
**335–337** *Keith Stephenson*
**338** *Adam Horan*
**339 and 340** *Keith Stephenson*
**342** *Rachel Calgaro*
**343** *Keith Stephenson*
**344 and 345** *Ed Butcher*

**346** *Keith Stephenson*
**347** *Luca Filho*
**348** *Ed Butcher*
**350** *Keith Stephenson*
**351** *Kyle E.Chambers*
**352 and 353** *Keith Stephenson*
**354** *Ed Butcher*
**355–357** *Keith Stephenson*
**360** *Dulux*
**361** *Christine Jamieson*
**362** *Thom Watson*
**363** *Karol Miles*
**365** *Thom Watson*
**366** *Paul Francis*
**367** *Keith Stephenson*
**368** *Paul Francis*
**369–373** *Keith Stephenson*
**374** *Mark Hampshire*
**375** *Kyle E.Chambers*
**376** *Keith Stephenson*
**378** *Karol Miles*
**379** *Keith Stephenson*
**380** *Helen Rickard*
**384–386** *Keith Stephenson*
**389** *Keith Stephenson*
**390** *Mark Hampshire*
**392 and 393** *Kyle E.Chambers*
**394 and 395** *Kyle E.Chambers*
**396** *Shannon Loewen*
**397** *Kyle E.Chambers*
**398** *Keith Stephenson*
**399** *Paul Sims*
**400 and 401** *Keith Stephenson*
**402** *Roy Caratozzolo III*
**407–424** *Courtesy of Adidas*
**425–428** *Charlie McRae*
**430–432** *Charlie McRae*
**433–441** *Keith Stephenson*

**Signals and Information**
444 Pete Ark
445 Karen Weese
447 Philipp Winterberg
448 Robert Sharl
449 Keith Stephenson
451 Paula Bailey
452 Paul McAleer
453 Keith Stephenson
454 By permission of Lee Sheridan
456 Keith Stephenson
459 and 460 Keith Stephenson
462 Paul McAleer
464 and 465 Keith Stephenson
467–470 Keith Stephenson
471–473 Keith Stephenson
476 Mark Hampshire
477 and 478 Keith Stephenson
486–488 Christine Jamieson
489 Vanessa della Cruz
490 and 491 Peter Ark
502 From the collection of
     www.simplonpc.co.uk
504–506 Tim Street - Porter
514–516 Dianne Calgaro
532 Sam at SUCK UK
545 and 546 Sam at SUCK UK
555 Bjorn Ehlert
559 and 560 Dana Damewood
562 Dana Damewood
564 Dana Damewood
567–579 Keith Stephenson
580 Toby Bradbury
581 Karol Miles
582–585 Keith Stephenson
588 and 589 Keith Stephenson
590 Paula Bailey
591 Keith Stephenson
593 Paula Bailey
602 Paul Francis
611 Keith Stephenson
612 Thom Watson
619 Paula Bailey
635 Kyle E.Chambers
636–639 Keith Stephenson
640 Paula Bailey
641 Keith Stephenson
642 Ashley Cameron

**Form and Function**
657 Keith Stephenson
658 Sam at SUCK UK
659 Karol Miles
660 Keith Stephenson
662 Paul Francis
664 Paul Francis
666 Keith Stephenson
669 Kyle E. Chambers
670 Lisa Brockmeier
671 Kyle E. Chambers
672 Paul McAleer
673 Paul McAleer
674–680 Keith Stephenson
682 Karol Miles
683 and 684 Keith Stephenson
685 Kyle E. Chambers
686–691 Keith Stephenson
692–703 Keith Stephenson
707 and 708 Keith Stephenson
710–712 Keith Stephenson
714 Ashley Cameron
715 Paul McAleer
716 Karol Miles
717 Paul Francis
718 Kyle E. Chambers
720 Keith Stephenson
721 Paul McAleer
722 Paul Duree
723 Keith Stephenson
724 Karol Miles
725 Keith Stephenson
726 Mark Hampshire
728 Paul McAleer

730 Paula Bailey
732 Karol Miles
733 Keith Stephenson
740 Keith Stephenson
741 and 742 Karol Miles
746 Keith Stephenson
751 Karol Miles
753–756 Keith Stephenson
757 Kyle E. Chambers
758 Spike
759 Keith Stephenson
761 and 762 Paula Bailey
763 Spike
764–766 Keith Stephenson
767 Paula Bailey
768 Karol Miles
769–771 Keith Stephenson
772 and 773 Karol Miles
774 Keith Stephenson
776 Keith Stephenson
777 Spike
779 and 780 Keith Stephenson
781 Paula Bailey
782 and 783 Keith Stephenson
784 Kyle E. Chambers
785 Spike
786 Keith Stephenson
787 Spike
792 Keith Stephenson
795 Keith Stephenson
797–799 Keith Stephenson
800 Carie Thompson
803 Karol Miles
804 Keith Stephenson

806 Keith Stephenson
808 Kyle E. Chambers
809 Keith Stephenson
812–814 Keith Stephenson
817 Paula Bailey
818 Keith Stephenson
819 Coutesy of Evisu International
820 Karol Miles
821 and 822 Keith Stephenson
849 Chris Moore
853 Ashley Cameron
854 Paul Francis
855 Karol Miles
858 and 859 Paul Francis
860 Karol Miles
862 Ella Doran
863 Keith Stephenson
866 Keith Stephenson
867 Michaela Forbes
868 Chris Brennan
870 Ella Doran book cover
872 Michaela Forbes
873 Kyle E. Chambers
874 Paula Bailey
875 Thom Watson
876 Matthew Lewis
877 Toby Bradbury
878–879 Paula Bailey
880–882 Keith Stephenson
883 Paula Bailey
884 and 885 Keith Stephenson
886 Paula Bailey

# Acknowledgments

Firstly, our special thanks to all at RotoVision for having the faith and confidence to let us loose on this project. Chris (master of the witty retort), April, and Tony—thanks for your support and patience in equal measures. Thanks especially to Luke for developing the idea and working so hard to get it off the ground in the first place.

Special thanks to Ben Kelly for stripe guidance and for writing an inspiring foreword. For disarming helpfulness, thanks to Daniel Buren and Sophie Streefkerk. Cheers to Scott Blake—his Web site, www.barcodeart.com, deserves huge recognition. We would have been lost without our design sources, and thanks in particular must go to Grace at design*sponge—a constant source of information and inspiration. Thanks also to Michel Pastoureau, whose book, *The Devil's Cloth*, has enlightened us and offered social and historical context. Also, we must thank Claire Hoult and the lovely staff and pupils of More House School—particularly Rebecca Skelly, Elvira Valdes, and Madelynn Lyon.

We are especially grateful for contributions, cooperation, and sheer hard graft to: Spike at Spike Ink, Emma Horley at Paul Smith, Michael Peters OBE, Brendan Martin, Ian Mankin, Saskia Boersma, Joanne Richardson, Liz Sowden at Thomas Pink, Beverly Collins, Simon at twentytwentyone, Todd Seidman, Laura at Brasserie Harkema, Marcello Minale, Rosemary Boon, Peter Chadwick, Wayne and Gerardine Hemingway, Sharon Elphick, Samuel E Rooker-Roberts, Abi Silvestre, Emma Haber at Nadine Johnson Inc, Sharilyn at Lovelydesign, Dr Ian West, Tom Dixon, Sarah Beerbohm, Michael Erdmann, The Cabin project, Katie McInnes, Miles at Purple PR, Nicola Pearce at DACS, Neil Taylor (www.motionandheart.co.uk), Chris and Rachel at the Original Breton Shirt Co, Andrea Dixon at The National Gallery of Canada, Nicola Shellswell, Steven Bateman, Wojtek Kozak, Lance Wyman, Luke J. Tornatzky, Liz Maryland, Stephen Gilmore, Drue Wagner, Tori at Camp Apparel, Ed Carpenter, Georgie Stout, Marius Rensen, Rob Hare, Sarah Boyd, Amy and Emma at agnès b, Meredith at Mole Architects, Carmen Marrero, Tony at REN (though we never got any free samples), Laura Slack and Shaggy, Eugenia, Sandrine Zerbib, Ros Hibbert, Lee Sheridan and Brotherhood of Man, Helen Parry, Darren Parry, Caroline, and the photogenic Ella and Jake.

The book simply wouldn't have happened without the generosity and enthusiasm of all our contributing photographers, so for skillful snapping and sheer volume of images, particular thanks must go to: Karol Miles, Paula Bailey, Paul Francis, Kyle E. Chambers, Robert Sharl, Carie Thompson, Kenji Szczepanski, Dominik Osterholt, cheeky Charlie McRae, Chris Brennan, Dianne Calgaro, Toby Bradbury, Thom Watson, and Ashley Cameron.

Finally, thanks to our friends and families who must be seeing stripes after putting up with months of obsessive rambling from us two.